Second Workshop on Privacy in Natural Language Processing (PrivateNLP2020)

Online
20 November 2020

ISBN: 978-1-7138-2001-7

Printed from e-media with permission by:

Curran Associates, Inc.
57 Morehouse Lane
Red Hook, NY 12571

Some format issues inherent in the e-media version may also appear in this print version.

Printed with permission by Curran Associates, Inc. (2021)

For permission requests, please contact the Association for Computational Linguistics at the address below.

Association for Computational Linguistics
209 N. Eighth Street
Stroudsburg, Pennsylvania 18360

Phone: 1-570-476-8006
Fax: 1-570-476-0860

acl@aclweb.org

Additional copies of this publication are available from:

Curran Associates, Inc.
57 Morehouse Lane
Red Hook, NY 12571 USA
Phone: 845-758-0400
Fax: 845-758-2633
Email: curran@proceedings.com
Web: www.proceedings.com

PrivateNLP2020

The Second Workshop on Privacy in Natural Language Processing

Nov 20, 2020
Online

Introduction

The PrivateNLP workshop aims to bring together practitioners and researchers from academia and industry to discuss the challenges and approaches to designing, building, verifying, and testing privacy preserving systems in the context of Natural Language Processing.

The workshop received 11 paper submissions this year and accepted 5 papers and one non-archival paper. These accepted papers cover membership inference attacks, text perturbation mechanisms, privacy mechanisms for language understanding tasks, automatic third-party identification in privacy policies, semantic similarity within privacy policies, and performance boosting of differentially private language models.

There are 5 invited speakers, Aaron Roth (University of Pennsylvania), Reza Shokri (National University of Singapore), Krishnaram Kenthapadi (Amazon AWS), Annabelle McIver (Macquarie University), and Mark Dras (Macquarie University). Each talk will cover different aspects of privacy-preserving NLP. We would like to thank the 33 Program Committee members who kindly reviewed the submissions, as well as the invited speakers, and the workshop co-organizers, Oluwaseyi Feyisetan (Amazon, USA), Sepideh Ghanavati (University of Maine, USA), Shervin Malmasi (Amazon, USA), and Patricia Thaine (University of Toronto, Canada).

Organizers:

Oluwaseyi Feyisetan, Amazon (USA)
Sepideh Ghanavati, University of Maine (USA)
Shervin Malmasi, Amazon (USA)
Patricia Thaine, University of Toronto (Canada)

Program Committee:

Aleksei Triastcyn, École Polytechnique Fédérale de Lausanne, (Switzerland)
Andreas Nautsch, EURECOM, (France)
Arne Köhn, Saarland University, (Germany)
Asma Eidhah Aloufi, Rochester Institute of Technology, (USA)
Balazs Pejo, Budapest University of Technology and Economics, (Hungary)
Benjamin Zi Hao Zhao, University of New South Wales, (Australia)
Briland Hitaj, SRI International, (USA)
Christian Weinert, Technische Universität Darmstadt, (Germany)
Congzheng Song, Cornell University, (USA)
Dinusha Vatsalan, Data61-CSIRO, (Australia)
Eleftheria Makri, Saxion University, (The Netherlands)
Elette Boyle, IDC Herzliya, (Israel)
Fang Liu, University of Notre Dame, (USA)
Gerald Penn, University of Toronto, (Canada)
Isar Nejadgholi, National Research Council, (Canada)
Jamie Hayes, University College London, (UK)
Jason Xue, University of Adelaide, (Australia)
Jaspreet Bhatia, (USA)
Julius Adebayom MIT, (USA)
Kambiz Ghazinour, State University of New York, (USA)
Ken Barker, University of Calgary, (Canada)
Liwei Song, Princeton University, (USA)
Luca Melis, Amazon, (USA)
Maximin Coavoux (University of Edinburgh), (UK)
Mitra Bokaei Hosseini, St. Mary's University, (USA)
Natasha Fernandes, Macquarie University, (Australia)
Nedelina Teneva, Amazon, (USA)
Peizhao Hu, Rochester Institute of Technology, (USA)
Sai Teja Peddinti, Google, (USA)
Shomir Wilson, Pennsylvania State University, (USA)
Tom Diethe, Amazon, (UK)
Travis Breaux, Carnegie Mellon University, (USA)
Xavier Ferrer, King's College London, (UK)

Invited Speaker:

Aaron Roth, University of Pennsylvania, (USA)
Reza Shokri, National University of Singapore, (Singapore)
Krishnaram Kenthapadi, Amazon AWS, (USA)
Annabelle McIver, Macquarie University, (Australia)
Mark Dras, Macquarie University, (Australia)

Table of Contents

Conference Program

8:45–9:00	*Welcome* Seyi Feyisetan
9:00–10:15	**Session 1**
9:00–9:45	***Invited Talk - Aaron Roth***
9:45–10:15	*On Log-Loss Scores and (No) Privacy* Abhinav Aggarwal, Zekun Xu, Oluwaseyi Feyisetan and Nathanael Teissier
10:30–12:15	**Session 2**
10:30–11:15	***Invited Talk 2 - Reza Shokri***
11:15–11:45	*A Differentially Private Text Perturbation Method Using Regularized Mahalanobis Metric* Zekun Xu, Abhinav Aggarwal, Oluwaseyi Feyisetan and Nathanael Teissier
11:45–12:15	*TextHide: Tackling Data Privacy in Language Understanding Tasks* Yangsibo Huang, Zhao Song, Danqi Chen, Kai Li and Sanjeev Arora
13:00–14:45	**Session 3**
13:00–13:45	***Invited Talk 3 - Mark Dras and Annabelle McIver***
13:45–14:15	*Identifying and Classifying Third-party Entities in Natural Language Privacy Policies* Mitra Bokaie Hosseini, Pragyan K C, Irwin Reyes and Serge Egelman
14:15–14:45	*Surfacing Privacy Settings Using Semantic Matching* Rishabh Khandelwal, Asmit Nayak, Yao Yao and Kassem Fawaz

No Day Set (continued)

15:00–17:00	**Session 4**
15:00–15:45	***Invited Talk 4 - Krishnaram Kenthapadi***
15:45–16:15	*Differentially Private Language Models Benefit from Public Pre-training* Gavin Kerrigan, Dylan Slack and Jens Tuyls
16:15–16:45	***Finding Paper***
16:45–17:00	*Closing Remarks* Seyi Feyisetan

On Primes, Log-Loss Scores and (No) Privacy

Abhinav Aggarwal
Amazon
Seattle, WA USA
aggabhin@amazon.com

Zekun Xu
Amazon
Seattle, WA USA
zeku@amazon.com

Oluwaseyi Feyisetan
Amazon
Seattle, WA USA
sey@amazon.com

Nathanael Teissier
Amazon
Arlington, VA USA
natteis@amazon.com

Abstract

A common metric for assessing the performance of binary classifiers is the Log-Loss score, which is a real number indicating the cross entropy distance between the predicted distribution over the labels and the true distribution (a point distribution defined by the ground truth labels). In this paper, we show that a malicious modeler, upon obtaining access to the Log-Loss scores on its predictions, can exploit this information to infer all the ground truth labels of arbitrary test datasets with full accuracy. We provide an efficient algorithm to perform this inference.

A particularly interesting application where this attack can be exploited is to breach privacy in the setting of Membership Inference Attacks. These attacks exploit the vulnerabilities of exposing models trained on customer data to queries made by an adversary. Privacy auditing tools for measuring leakage from sensitive datasets assess the total privacy leakage based on the adversary's predictions for datapoint membership. An instance of the proposed attack can hence, cause complete membership privacy breach, obviating any attack model training or access to side knowledge with the adversary. Moreover, our algorithm is agnostic to the model under attack and hence, enables perfect membership inference even for models that do not memorize or overfit. In particular, our observations provide insight into the extent of information leakage from statistical aggregates and how they can be exploited.

1 Introduction

Protecting customer privacy is of fundamental importance when training ML models on sensitive customer data. While explicit data de-identification and anonymization mechanisms can help protect privacy leakage to some extent, research has shown that this leakage can happen when models trained on customer data can be queried by an external entity (Homer et al., 2008; Sankararaman et al., 2009; Li et al., 2013; Shokri et al., 2017), or when statistical aggregates on the dataset are exposed (Dwork and Naor, 2010; Dwork et al., 2017).

Recently, it was shown that the knowledge of Log-Loss scores leaks information about true labels of test datapoints under some constraints on the prior knowledge on these labels (Whitehill, 2018). However, extracting meaningful information from these aggregates on arbitrary large datasets, while maintaining reasonable inference accuracy in a limited number of queries to a Log-Loss oracle remained an open problem, specially in cases when no prior knowledge is available. Moreover, the number of queries required by their algorithm scales with the size of the test dataset. We address this problem in this paper and provide multiple algorithms for optimal inference of arbitrarily many test labels in a single query using the exposed Log-Loss scores. This sheds insight into the extent of information leakage from this statistical aggregate and how it can be exploited to game a classification task, for example, in the context of data-mining competitions like Kaggle, KDDCup and ILSVRC Challenge (Russakovsky et al., 2015).

More concretely, consider the following scenario: you are tasked with a critical binary classification problem. The quality of your solution will be assessed through a performance score (Log-Loss) on an unknown test dataset. If you score the highest among all candidate solutions, then you win a significant cash prize. You are allowed only two attempts at the solution and the best of the two scores will be considered.

Is it possible to game this system in a way that your score is always the highest amongst all candidates, without even training any classifier?

We answer this in the affirmative by showing that the knowledge of only the size of the test dataset

Proceedings of the Second Workshop on Privacy in Natural Language Processing, pages 1–6
Online, Nov 20, 2020 ©2020 Association for Computational Linguistics
https://doi.org/10.18653/v1/P17

is enough to construct a scheme that can game any binary classifier that uses the Log-Loss metric to assess the quality of classification. This scheme is completely agnostic of the underlying classification task and hence, sheds light on how a malicious modeller can fake a perfect classifier by demonstrating zero test error. We assume that the oracle reports the scores truthfully on the entire dataset.

A particularly interesting application of our observation is for breaching membership privacy, where an attacker can query the model for inference on a set of datapoints and use these responses to infer what datapoints were used to train that model. Given blackbox access to a model and a data point x, this attack model is a binary classifier to infer the membership of x in the training dataset of the target model using its output on x – the more information this output reveals, the better this inference can be performed. Consequently, the accuracy of the attack depends on how well the adversary can capture the difference in model performance. Nonetheless, the popularity of this attack has made it a strong candidate for assessing privacy leakage of models trained on datasets containing sensitive information (Song and Shmatikov, 2019; Backes et al., 2016; Pyrgelis et al., 2017; Salem et al., 2018; Liu et al., 2019; Murakonda and Shokri, 2020). A successful attack can compromise the privacy of the users that contribute to the training dataset. Our results show that an oracle access to Log-Loss scores (for example, when using privacy auditors on sensitive datasets) enables full privacy breach in a single query[1].

Related Work In recent work, (Blum and Hardt, 2015) demonstrated how an attacker can estimate the test set labels in a competition setting with probability $2/3$. Similarly, and more related to our work, (Whitehill, 2016, 2018) showed how the knowledge of AUC and Log-Loss scores can be used to make inference on similar test sets by issuing multiple queries for these statistics. Our work extends the latter to optimize the number of queries. Similarly, through a Monte Carlo algorithm, (Matthews and Harel, 2013) show how knowing most of the test labels can help estimate the remaining labels upon gaining access to an empirical ROC curve. However, their algorithm is far from exact inference with no *apriori* information of the true labels.

We further observe that the theme of our work is related to two fields of research: adaptive data analysis, and protections of statistical aggregates using Differential Privacy (DP). In adaptive data analysis (Hardt and Ullman, 2014; Dwork et al., 2015), an attacker leverages multiple (adaptive) queries to sequentially construct a complete exploit (e.g., of a test set). Conversely, with DP (Dwork et al., 2006) the objective is to protect the aggregate statistics, such as those exploited by (Whitehill, 2016), from leaking information.

Log-Loss Metric We begin with reminding the reader of the definition of the Log-Loss metric on a given prediction vector with respect to a binary labeling of the datapoints in the test dataset.

Definition 1 (Log-Loss). *For a dataset $D = [d_1, \ldots, d_{|D|}]$, let $\ell \in \{0,1\}^{|D|}$ be a binary labeling and $\mathbf{x} = [x_1, \ldots, x_{|D|}] \in [0,1]^{|D|}$ be a vector of prediction scores. Let $g(\ell_i, x_i) = \ell_i \log_e x_i + (1 - \ell_i)\log_e(1 - x_i)$. Then, the Log-Loss (LL in short) for $\mathbf{x}$ with respect to ℓ is defined as $LL(\mathbf{x}, \ell) = -\frac{1}{|D|}\sum_{i=1}^{|D|} g(\ell_i, x_i)$.*

The definition easily generalizes for multi-class classifiers. A common variant is to ignore the normalization by $|D|$. Our constructions in this paper are scale-invariant.

2 Algorithms for Exact Inference using Log-Loss scores

In this section, we discuss multiple algorithms for single shot inference of all ground-truth labels using carefully constructed prediction vectors that help establish a 1-1 correspondence of the Log-Loss scores with the labelings of the test dataset. We, therefore, refer to the entity that performs such an inference as an *adversary*.

2.1 Inference using Twin Primes

Our first algorithm uses twin-primes, i.e. pairs of prime numbers within distance 2 of each other (see OEIS A001359 from `https://oeis.org/A001359`.). It has been conjectured that infinitely many such pairs exist (de Polignac, 1851). For a dataset of some finite size $|D| \geq 1$, we require $|D|$ such pairs. The main steps of our approach are

[1]Our paper can be viewed from two different lenses: exploiting, and information with the intent of protection. On one hand, our results demonstrate how to exploit performance metrics that are routinely vended from ML models, while on the other hand, they call to attention these vulnerabilities which might be currently under silent exploitation. Armed with this information, individuals and organizations which vend these seemingly innocuous aggregate metrics from their classification models, can grasp the potential scope of the information leakage that can result from this.

Algorithm 1: Inference on dataset $D = [d_1, \ldots, d_{|D|}]$ using Twin Primes

1. Let $5 \leq p_1 < \cdots < p_{|D|}$ be a sequence of (smallest) primes such that $p_i + 2$ is also a prime for all i.
2. Form the prediction vector for D as $\mathbf{x} = \left[\frac{p_1}{2+p_1}, \ldots, \frac{p_{|D|}}{2+p_{|D|}}\right]$.
3. Obtain the Log-Loss on $\mathbf{x}$ and use that to infer the ground-truth labels for D using Algorithm 2.

Algorithm 2: True Labels from Log-Loss

1. **Input:** Log-Loss score s
2. **Output:** True Labels for datapoints in D
3. Let $e^{s|D|} = p/q$ (lowest form) and $q = 2^m p_1 \cdots p_k$.
4. Find the set of (zero-indexed) locations I of primes $p_1 \ldots p_k$ in OEIS A001359.
5. Construct the labeling ℓ as follows: Insert 1 in indices specified by I, and 0s elsewhere.
6. Return ℓ.

outlined in Algorithm 1 and the following theorem proves its correctness.

Theorem 1. *If the Twin-Prime Conjecture holds, then for any dataset D, the Log-Loss scores returned by Algorithm 1 are in 1-1 correspondence with the binary labelings for datapoints in D.*

Proof. For a fixed D and labeling ℓ, it suffices to show that $-|D| \cdot LL(\mathbf{x}, \ell)$ takes all unique values. From Definition 1, it holds that:

$$-|D| \cdot LL(\mathbf{x}, \ell) = \log_e \left(\frac{2^{|D_0|} \prod_{d_j \in D_1} p_j}{(2+p_1) \cdots (2+p_{|D|})} \right).$$

Now, fix any two labelings ℓ_1 and ℓ_2 for D. If the number of zeros in them are different, then it is easy to see that $\mathbf{x}$ will give different Log-Loss scores on both of them, since the exponent of 2 in the numerator will be different for these two labelings and all other prime numbers being odd in the denominator, no common factors will exist to cancel this effect. If the number of zeros is the same, then observe that the following holds:

$$|D| \left(LL(\mathbf{x}, \ell_1) - LL(\mathbf{x}, \ell_2) \right) = \log_e \frac{\prod_{d_i \in D_1^{(2)}} p_i}{\prod_{d_j \in D_1^{(1)}} p_j},$$

where $D_1^{(2)}$ is the set of datapoints with label 1 in ℓ_2 (similarly for $D_1^{(1)}$). Now, since ℓ_1 and ℓ_2 are different, there must exist some index $1 \leq k \leq |D|$ for which $\ell_1(k) = 0$ and $\ell_2(k) = 1$. Thus, p_k will appear in the numerator but not in the denominator. Moreover, since the denominator is also a product of primes, it does not divide the numerator in this case, and hence, the difference $LL(\mathbf{x}, \ell_1) - LL(\mathbf{x}, \ell_2)$ is non-zero. □

As an example of this technique, assume $|D| = 2$. The primes we can use for this construction are 5 and 11, so that the prediction vectors can be set as $v_1 = [5/7, 2/7]$ and $v_2 = [11/13, 2/13]$. Then, the following lists the log-loss values for the prediction vector $\mathbf{x}^* = [5/7, 11/13]$ (as per Algorithm 1):

$$-2LL(\mathbf{x}^*, [0,0]) = \log_e \frac{2}{7} + \log_e \frac{2}{13} = \log_e \frac{4}{91}$$
$$-2LL(\mathbf{x}^*, [0,1]) = \log_e \frac{2}{7} + \log_e \frac{11}{13} = \log_e \frac{22}{91}$$
$$-2LL(\mathbf{x}^*, [1,0]) = \log_e \frac{5}{7} + \log_e \frac{2}{13} = \log_e \frac{10}{91}$$
$$-2LL(\mathbf{x}^*, [1,1]) = \log_e \frac{5}{7} + \log_e \frac{11}{13} = \log_e \frac{55}{91}$$

Our construction allows us to give an algorithm to determine the true labeling from the Log-Loss value, without having to consult a lookup table (see Algorithm 2). This follows from Gauss's Fundamental Theorem of Arithmetic (GFoA), that every positive integer is either a prime or is uniquely factorizable as a product of primes (Gauss, 1966). We assume that the Log-Loss score s is reported such that $e^{s|D|} = p/q$ is a rational number in its reduced form (i.e. with $q \neq 0$ and $\gcd(p,q) = 1$), and that, without loss of generality, the prediction vector was constructed using the first $|D|$ prime numbers, as specified in Algorithm 1.

As an example, suppose on a dataset of size 3, the Log-Loss s is reported such that $e^{3s} = 1729/170$. Note that this requirement of knowing $|D|$ is not necessary, since it is equal to the number of factors of the numerator of $e^{s|D|}$. Now, writing the denominator $170 = 2^1 \times 5 \times 17$, we note that there is 1 zero in the labeling, and the other two labels are one. From OEIS A001359, we note that 5 and 17 are the first and third prime numbers in the series (when we start counting from 5), respectively, and hence, the first and third datapoints must have labels one. Thus, we have inferred that the true labeling for D must be $[1,0,1]$.

2.2 Extension to Multiple Classes

A similar construction can be used to infer all true labels in a multi-class setting as well. For the One-vs-All approach, then it is trivial to see that the individual Log-Loss scores for each class reveal datapoints from that class. For the K-ary classifier approach (K being the number of classes), the following construction works: Let $p_1, \ldots, p_{|D|}$ be the first $|D|$ primes. For datapoint d_i, use the following prediction vector: $v_i = \left[1/\alpha_i, p_i/\alpha_i, \ldots, p_i^{K-1}/\alpha_i\right]$, where $\alpha_i = \sum_{j=0}^{K-1} p_i^j$, thus, forming the prediction matrix $v_D = \left[v_1, \ldots, v_{|D|}\right]$. Given the true labels $\ell \in \{1, \ldots, K\}^{|D|}$, it can be shown that the following holds:

$$-LL(v_D, \ell) + \sum_{j=1}^{K} \log_e \alpha_j = \log_e p_1^{\ell_1 - 1} \cdots p_{|D|}^{\ell_{|D|} - 1}.$$

This gives the required injection, since the sum on the left is constant for fixed K and $|D|$, and the product on the right is unique (following GFoA).

2.3 Inference using Binary Representations

In Algorithm 1, the main reason why we chose distinct primes was that when the denominator of $e^{s|D|}$ was factorized, the prime factors would uniquely define the locations of 1s in the binary labeling. The same 1-1 correspondence can be achieved by observing that the each binary labeling is also equivalent to a binary representation (base 2) of a natural number (see Algorithm 3). By using powers of 2 for only the indices corresponding to locations of 1s in the binary labeling, when the denominator is now factorized, it produces in the exponent of the 2 an integer, whose binary representation (when reversed) is exactly the same as the labeling. This also helps eliminate the dependence on the Twin Prime Conjecture. The following theorem establishes the correctness of our algorithm.

Theorem 2. *For any dataset D, the Log-Loss scores returned by Algorithm 3 are in 1-1 correspondence with the labelings for datapoints in D.*

Proof. Similar to the proof of Theorem 1, for a fixed D and labeling ℓ, it suffices to show that $d = |D| \cdot LL(\mathbf{x}, \ell)$ takes all unique values. Let I_1 be the set of indices in ℓ that have value 1. Now, since $x_i = \frac{2^{2^{i-1}}}{1+2^{2^{i-1}}}$, we can write the following:

$$d = \sum_{j=1}^{|D|} \log_e\left(1 + 2^{2^{j-1}}\right) - \frac{\sum_{i \in I_1} 2^{i-1}}{\log_2 e}.$$

Algorithm 3: Exact Inference using Binary Representations for $D = \left[d_1, \ldots, d_{|D|}\right]$.

Let $\alpha_i = 2^{2^{i-1}}$. Form the prediction vector for D as $\mathbf{x} = \left[\frac{\alpha_1}{1+\alpha_1}, \ldots, \frac{\alpha_{|D|}}{1+\alpha_{|D|}}\right]$.

Obtain the Log-Loss on $\mathbf{x}$ and use that to infer the true labels for D.

Thus, if $LL(\mathbf{x}, \ell_1) = LL(\mathbf{x}, \ell_2)$ for two distinct labelings ℓ_1 and ℓ_2, then from above, it is easy to see that this can only happen when $\sum_{i \in I_1^{(1)}} 2^{i-1} = \sum_{i \in I_1^{(2)}} 2^{i-1}$, where $I_1^{(j)}$ is the index set (similar to I_1) for labeling ℓ_j. Now, since every positive integer has a unique binary representation, this implies that $I_1^{(1)} = I_1^{(2)}$, which can only happen when the two labelings are the same. Moreover, note that since powers of 2 are always even, the product in the denominator of the equation above has no common factors with the numerator. Thus, each binary labeling of $\mathbf{x}$ gives a unique Log-Loss score. □

As an example, if the true labels for a dataset D containing four datapoints are $[1, 0, 1, 1]$, the exponent of 2 can be the natural number represented using the binary representation 1101, which is 13. Similarly, if the exponent observed is, say 18, then the corresponding binary representation is 10010, and hence, the true labels must be $[0, 1, 0, 0, 1]$.

3 Adapting to Fixed Precision Arithmetic

Can we design prediction vectors such that the Log-Loss scores are atleast some Δ apart from each other, where Δ is limited by the floating point precision on the machine used to simulate our inference algorithms?

For distinguishing scores with ϕ significant digits, since there are a total of 10^{ϕ} possible numeric values, the threshold value of separation is $\Delta \geq 10^{-\phi}$. If the separation in the scores is smaller than this value, then they cannot be distinguished. Inverting this inequality gives $\phi \geq \left\lceil \log_{10}\left(\frac{1}{\Delta}\right) \right\rceil$. For example, if one wishes to have the scores separated by $\Delta \geq 0.2$, then the minimum amount of precision required is $\lceil \log_{10} 5 \rceil = 1$. For $\Delta = 0.002$, we would need $\phi \geq \lceil \log_{10} 500 \rceil = 3$ digits.

We can reduce the requirement of a large precision by combining the AUC and Log-Loss scores, which is common in most practical situations where multiple performance metrics are evaluated to give a holistic overview of classifier inference. This way, even if they are individually not-unique but the tuple is unique for each labeling, exact inference can be done. For example, consider a dataset $D = [d_1, d_2, d_3]$ and the prediction vector $v = [0.2, 0.4, 0.6]$. Clearly, neither the AUC scores nor the Log-Loss scores are unique. However, if we consider the two scores together, the labels can be uniquely identified. Moreover, precision of only two significant digits is enough to make this decision.

A rough analysis tells us that with ϕ significant digits, there are $10^{\phi}(10^{\phi}+1)$ possible unique values in the AUC-Log-Loss tuple (the +1 is to take into account the case when AUC is Not-Defined). Using the pigeonhole principle, for any dataset D with $|D| = n$, a necessary condition for unique inference is that $2^n \leq 10^{\phi}(10^{\phi}+1)$, which gives $\phi \gtrsim \lceil 0.151n \rceil$. Conversely, with a precision of ϕ significant digits, one can only hope to uniquely identify labels for datasets of size at most $\lfloor \log_2 (10^{\phi}(10^{\phi}+1)) \rfloor \leq 7\phi$. We can recurse over the remaining points in the database in this situation, for exact inference in at most $\lceil n/6\phi \rceil$. For example, using the IEEE 754 double-precision binary floating-point format, which has at least 15 digits precision, at most $\left\lceil \frac{|D|}{90} \right\rceil$ queries suffice. In particular, 2 queries suffice for all datasets containing fewer than 180 datapoints.

4 Exact Membership Inference Attacks using a Log-Loss Oracle

Our observations provide insight into the extent of information leakage from statistical aggregates and how they can be exploited. A particularly interesting application is for designing stronger Membership Inference Attacks.

These attacks were first proposed to exploit the vulnerabilities of exposing models trained on customer data to queries by an adversary (Shokri et al., 2017), and later proposed to assess (1) data provenance by training language models on sensitive datasets (Song and Shmatikov, 2019) and (2) leakage from model outputs (Murakonda and Shokri, 2020). Such auditing techniques are becoming increasingly popular to quantify privacy leakage and because the underlying attack model is a binary classifier, aggregates like the Log-Loss scores will indicate the total privacy leakage based on the adversary's predictions.

The threat model we are interested in is the case when these aggregates are exposed to a malicious entity (adversary), in which case our analysis demonstrates that this additional information enables the adversary to craft malicious prediction vectors. The response to this query helps infer exactly which datapoints were used for training. Note that the adversary never queries the model under attack directly for prediction on any datapoints whatsoever. Moreover, the interaction with the model curator is similar to the interaction with the model interface in the attack proposed by (Shokri et al., 2017) in that the adversary seeks answers to queries that can help leak information about the training data. The only difference is the additional access to a Log-Loss oracle, which helps make our attack purely deterministic.

5 Conclusion and Future Work

In this paper, we demonstrated how a single Log-Loss query can enable exact inference of ground-truth labels of any number of test datapoints. This highlights the extent of information leakage from statistical aggregates, and in particular, that improperly constructed auditing tools may leak more information about the dataset than the leaky model they seek to expose. We see our work as a caution for such tools against reporting sensitive metrics.

An interesting question to ask is if other popular metrics (like precision, recall, AUC) used in the ML literature can be exploited for privacy leakage in a similar manner. In (Whitehill, 2019), an AUC-ROC oracle on the test dataset is used to deduce the true labels in at most $2|D|$ queries. This opens up opportunities to explore if exact inference on all datapoints is possible with one AUC query.

Yet another interesting question to ask is if exact inference is possible when the adversary learns only a bound on or an approximate value in each Log-Loss query it issues. Observe that by deciding the size of the test dataset, the adversary also fixes the number of possible values Log-Loss scores can take. In a typical scenario where the adversary has some prior knowledge about the amount by which the reported score differs from the actual value (see (Dwork et al., 2019) for an approach to add noise to the reported scores), this discrete set of possible scores can present a huge advantage – the adversary can perform inference over the most likely score under the constraint above. Nonetheless, a distribution over the labelings for the test set can be learnt to bound the inference error.

References

Michael Backes, Pascal Berrang, Mathias Humbert, and Praveen Manoharan. 2016. Membership privacy in microrna-based studies. In *Proceedings of the 2016 ACM SIGSAC Conference on Computer and Communications Security*, pages 319–330.

Avrim Blum and Moritz Hardt. 2015. The ladder: A reliable leaderboard for machine learning competitions. *arXiv preprint arXiv:1502.04585*.

Cynthia Dwork, Vitaly Feldman, Moritz Hardt, Toniann Pitassi, Omer Reingold, and Aaron Leon Roth. 2015. Preserving statistical validity in adaptive data analysis. In *Proceedings of the forty-seventh annual ACM symposium on Theory of computing*, pages 117–126.

Cynthia Dwork, Nitin Kohli, and Deirdre Mulligan. 2019. Differential privacy in practice: Expose your epsilons! *Journal of Privacy and Confidentiality*, 9(2).

Cynthia Dwork, Frank McSherry, Kobbi Nissim, and Adam Smith. 2006. Calibrating noise to sensitivity in private data analysis. In *Theory of cryptography conference*, pages 265–284. Springer.

Cynthia Dwork and Moni Naor. 2010. On the difficulties of disclosure prevention in statistical databases or the case for differential privacy. *Journal of Privacy and Confidentiality*, 2(1).

Cynthia Dwork, Adam Smith, Thomas Steinke, and Jonathan Ullman. 2017. Exposed! a survey of attacks on private data.

Carl Friedrich Gauss. 1966. *Disquisitiones arithmeticae*, volume 157. Yale University Press.

Moritz Hardt and Jonathan Ullman. 2014. Preventing false discovery in interactive data analysis is hard. In *2014 IEEE 55th Annual Symposium on Foundations of Computer Science*, pages 454–463. IEEE.

Nils Homer, Szabolcs Szelinger, Margot Redman, David Duggan, Waibhav Tembe, Jill Muehling, John V Pearson, Dietrich A Stephan, Stanley F Nelson, and David W Craig. 2008. Resolving individuals contributing trace amounts of dna to highly complex mixtures using high-density snp genotyping microarrays. *PLoS Genet*, 4(8):e1000167.

Ninghui Li, Wahbeh Qardaji, Dong Su, Yi Wu, and Weining Yang. 2013. Membership privacy: a unifying framework for privacy definitions. In *Proceedings of the 2013 ACM SIGSAC conference on Computer & communications security*, pages 889–900.

Gaoyang Liu, Chen Wang, Kai Peng, Haojun Huang, Yutong Li, and Wenqing Cheng. 2019. Socinf: Membership inference attacks on social media health data with machine learning. *IEEE Transactions on Computational Social Systems*, 6(5):907–921.

Gregory J Matthews and Ofer Harel. 2013. An examination of data confidentiality and disclosure issues related to publication of empirical roc curves. *Academic radiology*, 20(7):889–896.

Sasi Kumar Murakonda and Reza Shokri. 2020. Ml privacy meter: Aiding regulatory compliance by quantifying the privacy risks of machine learning. *arXiv preprint arXiv:2007.09339*.

Prince Alphonse de Polignac. 1851. *Recherches nouvelles sur les nombres premiers*.

Apostolos Pyrgelis, Carmela Troncoso, and Emiliano De Cristofaro. 2017. Knock knock, who's there? membership inference on aggregate location data. *arXiv preprint arXiv:1708.06145*.

Olga Russakovsky, Jia Deng, Hao Su, Jonathan Krause, Sanjeev Satheesh, Sean Ma, Zhiheng Huang, Andrej Karpathy, Aditya Khosla, Michael Bernstein, et al. 2015. Imagenet large scale visual recognition challenge. *International journal of computer vision*, 115(3):211–252.

Ahmed Salem, Yang Zhang, Mathias Humbert, Pascal Berrang, Mario Fritz, and Michael Backes. 2018. Ml-leaks: Model and data independent membership inference attacks and defenses on machine learning models. *arXiv preprint arXiv:1806.01246*.

Sriram Sankararaman, Guillaume Obozinski, Michael I Jordan, and Eran Halperin. 2009. Genomic privacy and limits of individual detection in a pool. *Nature genetics*, 41(9):965–967.

Reza Shokri, Marco Stronati, Congzheng Song, and Vitaly Shmatikov. 2017. Membership inference attacks against machine learning models. In *2017 IEEE Symposium on Security and Privacy (SP)*, pages 3–18. IEEE.

Congzheng Song and Vitaly Shmatikov. 2019. Auditing data provenance in text-generation models. In *Proceedings of the 25th ACM SIGKDD International Conference on Knowledge Discovery & Data Mining*, pages 196–206.

Jacob Whitehill. 2016. Exploiting an oracle that reports auc scores in machine learning contests. In *Thirtieth AAAI Conference on Artificial Intelligence*.

Jacob Whitehill. 2018. Climbing the kaggle leaderboard by exploiting the log-loss oracle. In *Workshops at the Thirty-Second AAAI Conference on Artificial Intelligence*.

Jacob Whitehill. 2019. How does knowledge of the auc constrain the set of possible ground-truth labelings? In *Proceedings of the AAAI Conference on Artificial Intelligence*, volume 33, pages 5425–5432.

A Differentially Private Text Perturbation Method Using a Regularized Mahalanobis Metric

Zekun Xu
Amazon
Seattle, WA USA
zeku@amazon.com

Abhinav Aggarwal
Amazon
Seattle, WA USA
aggabhin@amazon.com

Oluwaseyi Feyisetan
Amazon
Seattle, WA USA
sey@amazon.com

Nathanael Teissier
Amazon
Arlington, VA USA
natteis@amazon.com

Abstract

Balancing the privacy-utility tradeoff is a crucial requirement of many practical machine learning systems that deal with sensitive customer data. A popular approach for privacy-preserving text analysis is noise injection, in which text data is first mapped into a continuous embedding space, perturbed by sampling a spherical noise from an appropriate distribution, and then projected back to the discrete vocabulary space. While this allows the perturbation to admit the required metric differential privacy, often the utility of downstream tasks modeled on this perturbed data is low because the spherical noise does not account for the variability in the density around different words in the embedding space. In particular, words in a sparse region are likely unchanged even when the noise scale is large.

In this paper, we propose a text perturbation mechanism based on a carefully designed regularized variant of the Mahalanobis metric to overcome this problem. For any given noise scale, this metric adds an elliptical noise to account for the covariance structure in the embedding space. This heterogeneity in the noise scale along different directions helps ensure that the words in the sparse region have sufficient likelihood of replacement without sacrificing the overall utility. We provide a text-perturbation algorithm based on this metric and formally prove its privacy guarantees. Additionally, we empirically show that our mechanism improves the privacy statistics to achieve the same level of utility as compared to the state-of-the-art Laplace mechanism.

1 Introduction

Machine learning has been successfully utilized in a wide variety of real world applications including information retrieval, computer graphics, speech recognition, and text mining. Technology companies like Amazon, Google, and Microsoft already provide MLaaS (Machine Learning as a Service), where customers can input their datasets for model training and receive black-box prediction results as output. However, those datasets may contain personal and potentially sensitive information, which can be exploited to identify the individuals in the datasets, even if it has been anonymized (Sweeney, 1997; Narayanan and Shmatikov, 2008). Removing personally identifiable information is often inadequate, since having access to the summary statistics on the dataset has been shown to be sufficient to infer individual's membership in the dataset with high probability (Homer N, 2008; Sankararaman S., 2009; Dwork et al., 2015). Moreover, machine learning models themselves can reveal information on the training data. In particular, sophisticated deep neural networks for natural language processing tasks like next word prediction or neural machine translation, often tend to memorize their training data, which makes them vulnerable to leaking information about their training data (Shokri et al., 2017; Salem et al., 2018).

To provide a quantifiable privacy guarantee against such information leakage, Differential Privacy (DP) has been adopted as a standard framework for privacy-preserving analysis in statistical databases (Dwork et al., 2006; Dwork, 2008; Dwork et al., 2014). Intuitively, a randomized algorithm is differentially private if the output distributions from two neighboring databases are indistinguishable. However, a direct application of DP to text analysis can be too restrictive because it requires a lower bound on the probability of any word to be replaced by any other word in the vocabulary.

Metric differential privacy arises as a generalization of local differential privacy (Kasiviswanathan et al., 2011), which originated in protecting location privacy such that locations near the user's location are assigned with higher probability while those far away are given negligible probability

Proceedings of the Second Workshop on Privacy in Natural Language Processing, pages 7–17
Online, Nov 20, 2020 ©2020 Association for Computational Linguistics
https://doi.org/10.18653/v1/P17

(Andrés et al., 2013; Chatzikokolakis et al., 2013). In the context of privacy-preserving text analysis, metric differential privacy implies that the indistinguishability of the output distributions of any two words in the vocabulary is scaled by their distance, where the distance metrics used in the literature include Hamming distance (reduced to DP), Manhattan distance (Chatzikokolakis et al., 2015), Euclidean distance (Chatzikokolakis et al., 2013; Fernandes et al., 2019; Feyisetan et al., 2020), Chebyshev distance (Wagner and Eckhoff, 2018), hyperbolic distance (Feyisetan et al., 2019).

In this paper, we propose a novel privacy-preserving text perturbation method by adding an elliptical noise to word embeddings in the Euclidean space, where the scale of the noise is calibrated by the regularized Mahalanobis norm (formally defined in Section 3). We compare our method to the existing multivariate Laplace mechanism for privacy-preserving text analysis in the Euclidean space (Fernandes et al., 2019; Feyisetan et al., 2020). In both papers, text perturbation is implemented by adding a spherical noise sampled from multivariate Laplace distribution to the original word embedding. However, the spherical noise does not account for the structure in the embedding space. In particular, words in a sparse region are likely unchanged even when the scale of noise is large. This can potentially result in severe privacy breach when sensitive words do not get perturbed. To increase the substitution probability of words in sparse regions, the scale of noise has to be large in the multivariate Laplace mechanism, which will hurt the downstream machine learning utility.

We address this problem by adding an elliptical noise to word embeddings according to the covariance structure in the embedding space. The intuition is that given a fixed scale of noise, we want to stretch the noise equidistant contour in the direction so that the substitution probability of words in the sparse region is increased on average. Intuitively, this direction is the one that explains the largest variability in the word embedding vectors in the vocabulary. We prove the theoretical metric differential privacy guarantee of the proposed method. Furthermore, we use empirical analysis to show that the proposed method significantly improves the privacy statistics while achieves the same level of utility as compared to the multivariate Laplace mechanism. Our main contributions are as follows:

- We develop a novel Mahalanobis mechanism for differentially private text perturbation, which calibrates the elliptical noise by accounting for the covariance structure in the word embedding space.
- A theoretical metric differential privacy proof is provided for the proposed method.
- We compare the privacy statistics and utility results between our method and the multivariate Laplace Mechanism through experiments, which demonstrates that our method has significantly better privacy statistics while preserving the same level of utility.

2 Related Works

Privacy-preserving text analysis is a well-studied problem in the literature (Hill et al., 2016). One of the common approaches is to identify sensitive terms (like personally identifiable information) in a document and replace them with some more general terms (Cumby and Ghani, 2011; Anandan et al., 2012; Sánchez and Batet, 2016). Another line of research achieves text redaction by injecting additional words into the original text without detecting sensitive entities (Domingo-Ferrer et al., 2009; Pang et al., 2010; SáNchez et al., 2013). However, those methods are shown to be vulnerable to reidentification attacks (Petit et al., 2015).

In order to provide a quantifiable theoretical privacy guarantee, the differential privacy framework (Dwork, 2008) has been used for privacy-preserving text analysis. In the DPText model (Beigi et al., 2019), an element-wise univariate Laplace noise is added to the pre-trained auto-encoders to provide privacy for text representations. Another approach for privacy-preserving text perturbation is in the metric differential privacy framework (Andrés et al., 2013; Chatzikokolakis et al., 2013), an extended notion of local differential privacy (Kasiviswanathan et al., 2011), which adds noise to the pre-trained word embeddings. Metric differential privacy requires that the indistinguishability of the output distributions of any two words in the vocabulary be scaled by their distance, which reduces to differential privacy when Hamming distance is used (Chatzikokolakis et al., 2013). A hyperbolic distance metric (Feyisetan et al., 2019) was proposed to provide privacy by perturbing vector representations of words, but it requires specialized training of word embeddings in the high-dimensional hyperbolic space. For the word embeddings in the Euclidean space (Fernandes et al., 2019; Feyisetan et al., 2020), text perturbation is implemented by sampling independent spherical noise from multivariate Laplace distributions. The former work (Fernandes et al., 2019) subsequently used an Earth mover's metric to derive a Bag-of-Words representation on the text, whereas the latter (Feyisetan et al., 2020) directly worked on the word-level embeddings. Since we work with word embeddings in the Euclidean space, we compare our method to the multivariate Laplace mechanism for text perturbation in those two papers (Fernandes et al., 2019; Feyisetan et al., 2020).

Mahalanobis distance has been used as a sensitivity metric for differential privacy in functional data (Hall et al., 2012, 2013) and differentially private outlier analysis (Okada et al., 2015). Outside the realm of text analysis, Mahalanobis distance is a common tool in cluster analysis, pattern recognition, and anomaly detection (De Maesschalck et al., 2000; Xiang et al., 2008; Warren et al., 2011; Zhao et al., 2015; Zhang et al., 2015).

3 Methodology

We begin by formally defining Euclidean norm and the regularized Mahalanobis norm.

Definition 1 (Euclidean Norm). *For any vector $x \in \mathbb{R}^m$, its Euclidean norm is:* $\|x\|_2 = \sqrt{x^\intercal x}$.

Definition 2 (Mahalanobis Norm). *For any vector $x \in \mathbb{R}^m$, and a positive definite matrix Σ, its Mahalanobis norm is:*

$$\|x\|_M = \sqrt{x^\intercal \Sigma^{-1} x}.$$

Definition 3 (Regularized Mahalanobis Norm). *For any vector $x \in \mathbb{R}^m$, $\lambda \in [0, 1]$, and a positive definite matrix Σ, its regularized Mahalanobis norm is:*

$$\|x\|_{RM} = \sqrt{x^\intercal \{\lambda\Sigma + (1-\lambda)I_m\}^{-1} x}.$$

From the definitions above, λ can be considered as a tuning parameter. When $\lambda = 0$, the regularized Mahalanobis norm reduces to the Euclidean norm; when $\lambda = 1$, the regularized norm reduces to the Mahalanobis norm (Mahalanobis, 1936)

Note that for any $\eta > 0$, the trajectory of $\{y \in \mathbb{R}^m : \|y - x\|_2 = \eta\}$ is spherical, whereas the trajectory of $\{y \in \mathbb{R}^m : \|y - x\|_{RM} = \eta\}$ is elliptical unless $\lambda = 0$. We will exploit this key difference in the geometry of equidistant contour between the Euclidean norm and the regularized Mahalanobis norm to motivate our text perturbation method. The proposed regularized Mahalanobis norm is a type of shrinkage estimator (Daniels and Kass, 2001; Schäfer and Strimmer, 2005; Couillet and McKay, 2014), which is commonly used to estimate the covariance matrix of high-dimensional vectors so as to ensure the stability of the estimator. The matrix Σ in the regularized Mahalanobis norm controls the direction to which the equidistant contour in the noise distribution is stretched, while the parameter λ controls the degree of the stretch.

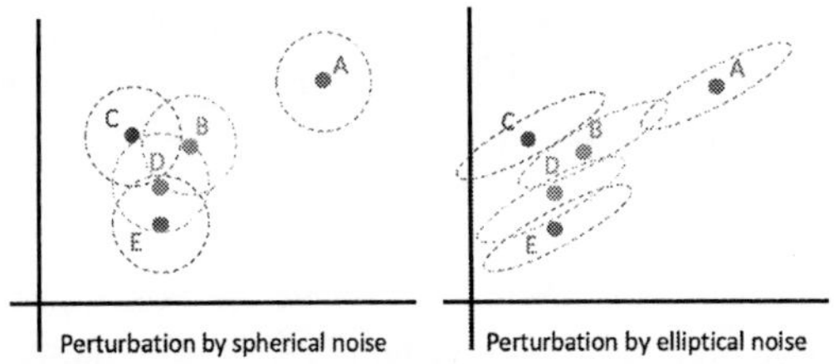

Figure 1: **Left:** dotted trajectories represent perturbation by spherical noise in multivariate Laplace mechanism. **Right:** dotted trajectories represent perturbation by elliptical noise in proposed Mahalanobis mechanism. The scale of noise is the same in both plots.

Definition 4 (Metric Differential Privacy.). *For any $\epsilon > 0$, a randomized algorithm $M : \mathcal{X} \to \mathcal{Y}$ satisfies $\epsilon\ d_\mathcal{X}$−privacy if for any $x, x' \in \mathcal{X}$ and $y \in \mathcal{Y}$, the following holds:*

$$\frac{\Pr\{M(x) = y\}}{\Pr\{M(x') = y\}} \leq \exp\{\epsilon d(x, x')\}.$$

Metric differential privacy ($d_\mathcal{X}$−privacy) originated in privacy-preserving geolocation studies (Andrés et al., 2013; Chatzikokolakis et al., 2013), where the metric d is Euclidean distance. It has been extended to quantifying privacy guarantee in text analysis, which states that for any two words w, w' in the vocabulary $\mathcal{W}$, the likelihood ratio of observing any $\hat{w} \in \mathcal{W}$ is bounded by $\epsilon d(w, w')$, where $d(w, w') = \|\phi(w) - \phi(w')\|_2$ for an embedding function $\phi : \mathcal{W} \to \mathbb{R}^m$.

The multivariate Laplace mechanism (Fernandes et al., 2019; Feyisetan et al., 2020) perturbs the word embedding $\phi(w)$ by adding a random spherical noise Z sampled from density $f_Z(z) \propto e^{\epsilon\|z\|_2}$, and then find the nearest neighbor in the embedding space as the output of the mechanism.

The left panel in Figure 1 illustrates the text perturbation by spherical noise in the multivariate Laplace mechanism. Here A is in the sparse region in the two-dimensional embedding space.

Given the privacy budget ϵ, A has a small probability of being substituted by other words because its expected perturbation (dotted trajectory) still has itself as the nearest neighbor. The right panel in Figure 1 shows text perturbation in the proposed Mahalanobis mechanism, where the word embeddings are redacted by an elliptical noise at the same privacy budget ϵ. The matrix Σ is taken to be the sample covariance matrix of the word embeddings scaled by the mean sample variance, so that the noise contour is stretched toward the direction that explains the largest variability in the embedding space. The purpose of the scaling step is to ensure that the scale of the elliptical noise is the same as the scale of the spherical noise. By transforming the spherical noise contour into an elliptical contour, we increase the substitution probability of A in the sparse region, thus improving the privacy guarantee. Meanwhile, since the scale of noise does not change, the utility is preserved at the same level. This is an illustrative example demonstrating the intuition and motivation of the proposed Mahalanobis mechanism.

Our proposed Mahalanobis mechanism for text perturbation shares the same general structure as the multivariate Laplace mechanism. The key difference is that the spherical noise $f_Z(z) \propto \exp(\epsilon\|z\|_2)$ in the multivariate Laplace mechanism is replaced by the elliptical noise sampled from density $f_Z(z) \propto \exp(-\epsilon\|z\|_{\mathsf{RM}})$, which can be efficiently performed via Algorithm 1.

An overview for the proposed Mahalanobis mechanism is presented in Algorithm 2. When $\lambda = 0$, the proposed Mahalanobis mechanism reduces to the multivariate Laplace mechanism. A heuristic method for choosing the tuning parameter λ is to find the value of λ that maximizes the improvement in the privacy guarantee while maintaining the same level of utility. This can be done through empirical privacy and utility experiments as described in Section 5. The input Σ in Algorithm 2 is computed by scaling the sample covariance matrix of the word embeddings by the mean sample variance so as to guarantee that the trace of Σ equals the trace of I_m. Since Σ is a scaled counterpart of the sample covariance matrix, it will stretch the elliptical noise toward the direction with the largest variability in the word embedding space, which maximizes the overall expected probability of words being substituted. We remark that in order to maximize the substitution probability for each individual word, a personalized covariance matrix Σ_w can be computed in the neighborhood of each word. This is beyond the scope of this paper and we leave it as future work.

4 Theoretical Properties

Lemma 1. *The random variable Z returned from Algorithm 1 has a probability density function of the form $f_Z(z) \propto \exp(-\epsilon\|z\|_{\mathsf{RM}})$.*

Proof. Define $U = YX$. Note that conditional on Y, U follows a uniform distribution on a sphere with radius y in the $m-$dimensional space, which implies $f_{U|Y}(u|y) \propto 1/y^{m-1}$ when $\sum_{i=1}^m u_i^2 = y^2$ and 0 otherwise. Therefore,

$$\begin{aligned} f_U(u) &= \int f_{U|Y}(u|y) f_Y(y)\delta(y = \|u\|_2)dy \\ &\propto \int \frac{1}{y^{m-1}} \frac{\epsilon^m}{\Gamma(m)} y^{m-1} e^{-\epsilon y}\delta(y = \|u\|_2)dy \\ &\propto e^{-\epsilon\sqrt{u^\intercal u}}, \end{aligned}$$

where $\delta(\cdot)$ is the Dirac delta function. Since $Z = \{\lambda\Sigma + (1-\lambda)I_m\}^{1/2}U$, which is well-defined because $\lambda \in [0, 1]$ and Σ is positive definite, it follows that:

$$f_Z(z) \propto \exp\left(-\epsilon\sqrt{z^\intercal\{\lambda\Sigma + (1-\lambda)I_m\}^{-1}z}\right),$$

The result in the lemma follows by definition. □

Theorem 1. *For any given $\epsilon > 0$ and $\lambda \in [0, 1]$, the Mahalanobis mechanism from Algorithm 2 satisfies ϵ d_χ-privacy with respect to the Regularized Mahalanobis Norm.*

Proof. It suffices to show that for any strings $s = [w_1 \ldots w_n]$, $s' = [w_1' \ldots w_n']$, $\hat{s} = [\hat{w}_1 \ldots \hat{w}_n]$, $\epsilon > 0$, $\lambda \in [0, 1]$, and positive definite matrix Σ,

$$\frac{\Pr\{M(s) = \hat{s}\}}{\Pr\{M(s') = \hat{s}\}} \le e^{\epsilon\sum_{i=1}^n \|\phi(w_i) - \phi(w_i')\|_{\mathsf{RM}}},$$

where $M : \mathcal{W}^n \to \mathcal{W}^n$ is the Mahalanobis mechanism and $\phi : \mathcal{W} \to \mathbb{R}^m$ is the embedding function.

We begin by showing that for any $w, w', \hat{w} \in \mathcal{W}$, it holds that the probability $\Pr\{M(w) = \hat{w}\}$ is at most $e^{\epsilon\|\phi(w) - \phi(w')\|_{\mathsf{RM}}}$ times the probability $\Pr\{M(w') = \hat{w}\}$. We define $C_{\hat{w}} = \{v \in \mathbb{R}^m : \|v - \phi(\hat{w})\|_2 < \min_{w \in \mathcal{W}\backslash\hat{w}} \|v - \phi(w)\|_2\}$ be the set of vectors v that are closer to $\hat{w}$ than any other

Algorithm 1: Sampling from $f_Z(z) \propto \exp(-\epsilon \|z\|_{\mathsf{RM}})$

Input: Dimension m, a positive definite matrix Σ, tuning parameter $\lambda \in [0, 1]$
Sample an m-dimensional random vector N from a multivariate normal distribution with mean zero and identity covariance matrix.
Normalize $X = N / \|N\|_2$.
Sample Y from a Gamma distribution with shape parameter m and scale parameter $1/\epsilon$.
Return $Z = Y \cdot \{\lambda\Sigma + (1-\lambda)I_m\}^{1/2} X$.

Algorithm 2: The Mahalanobis Mechanism

```
Input: String s = w_1 w_2 ... w_n, privacy parameter ε > 0, scaled sample covariance matrix Σ,
    tuning parameter λ ∈ [0, 1]
for i ∈ {1, ..., n} do
    Sample Z from f_Z(z) ∝ exp(−ε‖z‖_RM) using Algorithm 1.
    Obtain the perturbed embedding φ̂_i = φ(w_i) + Z.
    Replace w_i with ŵ_i = argmin_{w∈W} ‖φ(w) − φ̂_i‖_2.
return s̃ = ŵ_1 ŵ_2 ... ŵ_n.
```

word in the embedding space. Let Z be sampled from $f_Z(z) \propto \exp(-\epsilon\|z\|_{\mathsf{RM}})$ by Algorithm 1,

$$\Pr\{M(w) = \hat{w}\} = \Pr\{\phi(w) + Z \in C_{\hat{w}}\}$$
$$= \int_{C_{\hat{w}}} f_Z(v - \phi(w))\, dv = \int_{C_{\hat{w}}} e^{-\epsilon\|v-\phi(w)\|_{\mathsf{RM}}} dv,$$

where the last step follows from Lemma 1. Since Σ is positive definite, it admits a spectral decomposition $\Sigma = Q\Lambda Q^\intercal$, where $Q^\intercal = Q^{-1}$, and Λ is a diagonal matrix with positive entries $\xi_1, \ldots, \xi_m$. Then we can rewrite $\{\lambda\Sigma + (1-\lambda)I_m\}^{-1} = Q\Omega Q^\intercal$, where $\Omega^{-1} = \lambda\Lambda + (1-\lambda)I_m$. Define $\tilde{v} = \Omega^{1/2}Q^\intercal v$ and $\tilde{\phi}(w) = \Omega^{1/2}Q^\intercal\phi(w)$. By the triangle inequality, the following hold:

$$\begin{aligned}
&e^{-\epsilon\sqrt{\{v-\phi(w)\}^\intercal\{\lambda\Sigma+(1-\lambda)I_d\}^{-1}\{v-\phi(w)\}}}\\
=&e^{-\epsilon\sqrt{\{v-\phi(w)\}^\intercal Q\Omega^{1/2}\Omega^{1/2}Q^\intercal\{v-\phi(w)\}}}\\
=&e^{-\epsilon\|\tilde{v}-\tilde{\phi}(w)\|_2}\\
=&\frac{e^{-\epsilon\|\tilde{v}-\tilde{\phi}(w')\|_2}}{e^{-\epsilon\|\tilde{v}-\tilde{\phi}(w')\|_2}}e^{-\epsilon\|\tilde{v}-\tilde{\phi}(w)\|_2}\\
\le&e^{-\epsilon\|\tilde{v}-\tilde{\phi}(w')\|_2}e^{\epsilon\|\tilde{\phi}(w)-\tilde{\phi}(w')\|_2}\\
=&e^{-\epsilon\|v-\phi(w')\|_{\mathsf{RM}}}e^{\epsilon\|\phi(w)-\phi(w')\|_{\mathsf{RM}}}.
\end{aligned}$$

The probability ratio is computed by:

$$\frac{\Pr\{M(w)=\hat{w}\}}{\Pr\{M(w')=\hat{w}\}} = \frac{\int_{C_{\hat{w}}} e^{-\epsilon\|v-\phi(w)\|_{\mathsf{RM}}} dv}{\int_{C_{\hat{w}}} e^{-\epsilon\|v-\phi(w')\|_{\mathsf{RM}}} dv} \le e^{\epsilon\|\phi(w)-\phi(w')\|_{\mathsf{RM}}}.$$

Finally, since each word in the string is processed independently,

$$\begin{aligned}
\frac{\Pr(M(s)=\hat{s})}{\Pr(M(s')=\hat{s})} &= \prod_{i=1}^{n}\left(\frac{\Pr(M(w_i)=\hat{w}_i)}{\Pr(M(w_i')=\hat{w}_i)}\right)\\
&\le \prod_{i=1}^{n} e^{\epsilon\|\phi(w_i)-\phi(w_i')\|_{\mathsf{RM}}}\\
&\le e^{\epsilon\sum_{i=1}^{n}\|\phi(w_i)-\phi(w_i')\|_{\mathsf{RM}}}. \square
\end{aligned}$$

Next, we relate the proved theoretical guarantee of the Mahalanobis mechanism to that of the multivariate Laplace mechanism (Fernandes et al., 2019; Feyisetan et al., 2020), which enjoys metrical differential privacy guarantee with respect to the Euclidean metric. The following lemma will help establish our result.

Lemma 2. *Let $v \in \mathbb{R}^2$ and $m = trace(\Sigma)$. Let $c > 0$ be a lower bound on the smallest eigenvalue of Σ. Then, the following bounds hold:*

$$\frac{||v||_2}{\sqrt{\lambda m + 1 - \lambda}} \le ||v||_{RM} \le \frac{||v||_2}{\sqrt{\lambda c + 1 - \lambda}}.$$

Proof. Since Σ is positive definite, it admits a spectral decomposition $\Sigma = Q\Lambda Q^\intercal$, where $Q^\intercal = Q^{-1}$, and Λ is a diagonal matrix with eigenvalues $\xi_1, \ldots, \xi_m$. Since by assumption of the minimum eigenvalue greater than $c > 0$, and that $trace(\Sigma) = \sum_{i=1}^{m} \xi_i = m$, we have $\xi_i \in (c, m)$ for $i = 1, \ldots, m$. Then, the eigenvalues for $\{\lambda\Sigma + (1-\lambda)I_m\}^{-1}$ are $\frac{1}{\lambda\xi_1+1-\lambda}, \ldots, \frac{1}{\lambda\xi_m+1-\lambda}$, which are between $\frac{\epsilon}{\lambda m+1-\lambda}$ and $\frac{\epsilon}{\lambda c+1-\lambda}$. Then for any vector $v \in \mathbb{R}^m$,

$$
\begin{aligned}
\|v\|^2_{\mathsf{RM}} =& v^\mathsf{T}\{\lambda\Sigma + (1-\lambda)I_m\}^{-1}v \\
=& \sum_{i=1}^{m} \frac{1}{\lambda\xi_i + 1 - \lambda}(q_i^\mathsf{T} v)^2 \\
\leq& \frac{1}{\lambda c + 1 - \lambda}\sum_{i=1}^{m}(q_i^\mathsf{T} v)^2 = \frac{\|v\|_2^2}{\lambda c + 1 - \lambda},
\end{aligned}
$$

where $\sum_{i=1}^{m}(q_i^\mathsf{T} v)^2 = \|Q^\mathsf{T} v\|_2^2 = \|v\|_2^2$. Similarly, we can show that $\|v\|^2_{\mathsf{RM}} \geq \frac{1}{\lambda m+1-\lambda}\|v\|_2^2$, so the result follows immediately. □

The lemma below then follows.

Lemma 3. *Assume $trace(\Sigma) = m$ and the minimum eigenvalue of Σ is greater than c for some constant $c > 0$, then for any $w, w' \in \mathcal{W}$, then*

$$
\begin{aligned}
&\exp\left(\epsilon\|\phi(w) - \phi(w')\|_{RM}\right) \\
\leq& \exp\left(\frac{\epsilon}{\sqrt{\lambda c + 1 - \lambda}}\|\phi(w) - \phi(w')\|_2\right), \quad \textit{and} \\
&\exp\left(\epsilon\|\phi(w) - \phi(w')\|_{RM}\right) \\
\geq& \exp\left(\frac{\epsilon}{\sqrt{\lambda m + 1 - \lambda}}\|\phi(w) - \phi(w')\|_2\right).
\end{aligned}
$$

The fact that the probability ratio as a function of $\|\cdot\|_{\mathsf{RM}}$ can be sandwiched by lower and upper bounds as functions of $\|\cdot\|_2$ shows the noise scale ϵ is comparable between the Mahalanobis mechanism and multivariate Laplace mechanism.

5 Experiments

We empirically compare the proposed Mahalanobis mechanism and the existing multivariate Laplace mechanism in both privacy experiments and utility experiments on the following two datasets (more details in Appendix A):

- **Twitter Dataset**. This is a publicly available Kaggle competition dataset (`https://www.kaggle.com/c/nlp-getting-started`), which contains 7,613 tweets, each with a label indicating whether the tweet describes a disaster event (43% disaster).
- **SMSSpam Dataset**. This is a publicly available dataset from the UCI machine learning repository (`https://archive.ics.uci.edu/ml/datasets/SMS+Spam+Collection`), which contains 5,574 (13% spam) SMS labeled messages collected for mobile phone spam research (Almeida et al., 2011).

5.1 Privacy experiments

In the privacy experiments, we compare the Mahalanobis mechanism with the multivariate Laplace mechanism on the following two privacy statistics:

1. $N_w = \Pr\{M(w) = w\}$, which is the probability of the word not getting redacted in the mechanism. This is approximated by counting the number of times an input word w does not get replaced by other words after running the mechanism for 100 times.

2. $S_w = |\{w' \in \mathcal{W} : \Pr\{M(w) = w'\} \geq \eta|$, which is the number of distinct words that have a probability greater than η of being the output of $M(w)$. This is approximated by counting the number of distinct substitutions for an input word w after running the mechanism for 100 times.

We note that N_w and S_w have been previously used in privacy-preserving text analysis literature to qualitatively characterize the privacy guarantee (Feyisetan et al., 2019, 2020). We make the following connection between the privacy statistics (N_w and S_w) with the DP privacy budget ϵ: a smaller ϵ corresponds to a stronger privacy guarantee by adding a larger scale ($1/\epsilon$) of noise in the mechanism, which leads to fewer unperturbed words (lower N_w) and more diverse outputs for each word (higher S_w). For any fixed noise scale of $1/\epsilon$, the mechanism with a better privacy guarantee will have a lower value of N_w and higher value of S_w.

In Figure 2 and 3, we summarize how the 5th, 50th, and 95th percentiles of N_w and S_w change in different configurations of the mechanisms using the 300-d FastText embedding (Bojanowski et al., 2017). The vocabulary set includes 28,596 words in the vocabulary union from the two real datasets. For all 5th, 50th, and 95th percentiles, the Mahalanobis mechanism has a lower value of N_w and a higher value of S_w as compared to the multivariate Laplace mechanism, which indicates an improvement in privacy statistics.

Table 1 and 2 compare the mean and standard deviation of N_w and S_w across different settings. The mean N_w converges to 0 as ϵ decreases and converges to 100 as ϵ increases. An opposite trend is observed for S_w, which is as expected. In the middle range of privacy budget ($\epsilon = 5, 10, 20$), the proposed Mahalanobis mechanism has significantly lower values of N_w and higher values of S_w, where

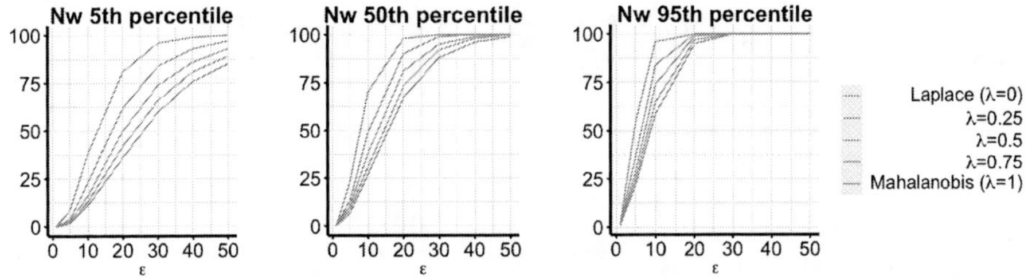

Figure 2: Percentiles for N_w (number of times an input word w does not change) for 300-d FastText embedding over 100 repetitions. The Mahalanobis mechanism has lower values of N_w than the Laplace mechanism.

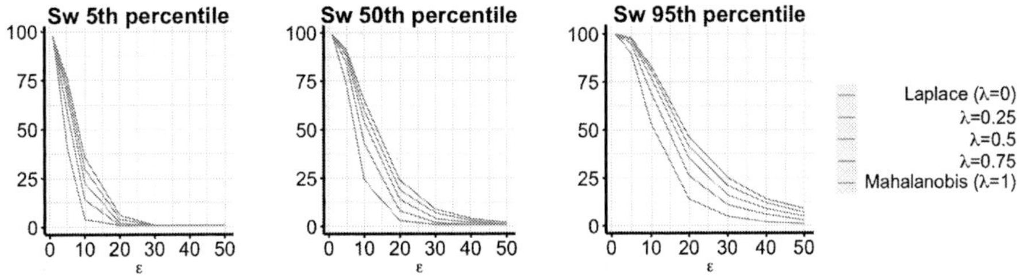

Figure 3: Percentiles for S_w (number of distinct substitutions for an input word w) for 300-d FastText embedding over 100 repetitions. The Mahalanobis mechanism has higher values of S_w than the Laplace mechanism.

ϵ	1	5	10	20	40
Laplace ($\lambda = 0$)	0.19±0.46	26.89±14.49	68.93±17.97	95.28±6.46	99.85±0.68
$\lambda = 0.25$	0.15±0.41	16.66±10.53	50.31±18.68	86.34±12.41	98.69±2.81
$\lambda = 0.5$	0.13±0.38	12.68±8.60	40.40±17.41	78.44±15.40	96.91±4.88
$\lambda = 0.75$	0.12±0.36	10.46±7.49	34.14±16.03	71.81±17.00	94.85±6.79
Mahalanobis ($\lambda = 1$)	0.10±0.35	8.97±6.74	29.73±14.83	66.24±17.90	92.80±8.31

Table 1: Mean ± Standard Deviation for N_w for 300-d FastText embedding. For $\epsilon = 5, 10, 20$, the Mahalanobis mechanism has significantly lower values of mean N_w than the Laplace mechanism, where statistical significance is established by comparing the 95% confidence intervals in the form of $mean \pm 1.96 \times std/\sqrt{100}$.

ϵ	1	5	10	20	40
Laplace ($\lambda = 0$)	99.23±0.87	70.27±15.07	25.82±15.06	4.53±4.56	1.13±0.55
$\lambda = 0.25$	99.18±0.90	81.42±11.12	42.59±16.56	10.31±8.08	1.93±1.80
$\lambda = 0.5$	99.07±0.96	85.69±9.10	52.26±15.96	15.66±10.18	2.98±2.83
$\lambda = 0.75$	98.95±1.03	88.08±7.96	58.66±15.13	20.38±11.46	4.16±3.75
Mahalanobis ($\lambda = 1$)	98.88±1.04	89.58±7.17	63.28±14.25	24.60±12.37	5.32±4.51

Table 2: Mean ± Standard Deviation for S_w for 300-d FastText embedding. For $\epsilon = 5, 10, 20$, the Mahalanobis mechanism has significantly higher values of mean S_w than the Laplace mechanism, where statistical significance is established by comparing the 95% confidence intervals in the form of $mean \pm 1.96 \times std/\sqrt{100}$.

the statistical significance is established by comparing the 95% confidence intervals for mean N_w and S_w in the form of $mean \pm 1.96 \times std/\sqrt{100}$. While the scale of the noise is controlled to be the same across settings, the probability that a word does not change becomes smaller and the number of distinct substitutions becomes larger in our proposed mechanism. This shows the advantage of the Mahalanobis mechanism over the multivariate Laplace mechanism in privacy statistics.

The results are qualitatively similar when we repeat the same set of privacy experiments using the 300-d GloVe embeddings (Pennington et al., 2014). As can be seen in Figure 4, Figure 5, Table 3, and Table 4), the Mahalanobis mechanism has lower values of N_w and higher values of S_w compared

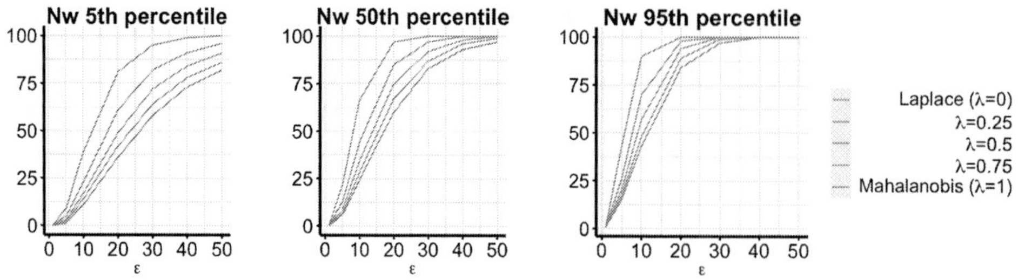

Figure 4: Percentiles for N_w (number of times an input word w does change) for 300-d GloVe embedding over 100 repetitions. The Mahalanobis mechanism has lower values of N_w than the Laplace mechanism.

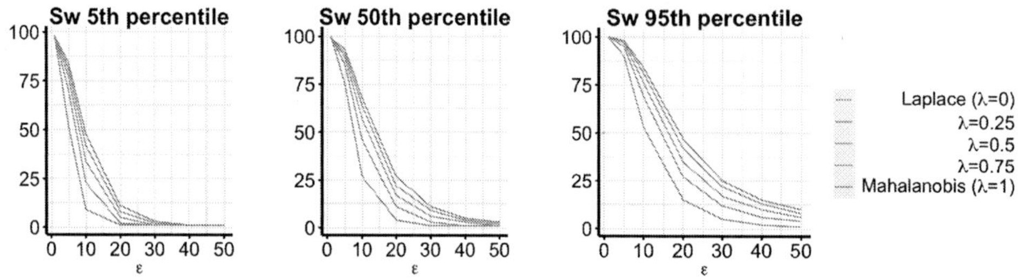

Figure 5: Percentiles for S_w (number of distinct substitutions for an input word w) for 300-d GloVe embedding over 100 repetitions. The Mahalanobis mechanism has higher values of S_w than the Laplace mechanism.

ϵ	1	5	10	20	40
Laplace ($\lambda = 0$)	0.16±0.41	23.71±10.69	65.29±15.53	94.49±6.48	99.81±0.74
$\lambda = 0.25$	0.11±0.34	13.82±6.89	44.83±14.17	83.17±11.61	98.22±3.31
$\lambda = 0.5$	0.09±0.31	10.20±5.57	34.91±12.12	73.78±13.59	95.85±5.56
$\lambda = 0.75$	0.08±0.29	8.16±4.87	28.97±10.72	66.29±14.35	93.26±7.30
Mahalanobis ($\lambda = 1$)	0.08±0.28	6.81±4.36	24.90±9.60	60.27±14.54	90.60±8.65

Table 3: Mean ± Standard Deviation for N_w for 300-d GloVe embedding. For $\epsilon = 5, 10, 20$, the Mahalanobis mechanism has significantly lower values of mean N_w than the Laplace mechanism, where statistical significance is established by comparing the 95% confidence intervals in the form of $mean \pm 1.96 \times std/\sqrt{100}$.

ϵ	1	5	10	20	40
Laplace ($\lambda = 0$)	99.46±0.74	73.20±11.60	28.56±13.61	5.18±4.64	1.16±0.62
$\lambda = 0.25$	99.45±0.73	84.30±7.62	46.08±13.98	12.12±7.69	2.21±2.02
$\lambda = 0.5$	99.38±0.79	88.39±6.08	56.07±12.92	17.96±9.33	3.55±3.06
$\lambda = 0.75$	99.30±0.83	90.71±5.27	62.69±11.84	23.11±10.42	4.94±3.90
Mahalanobis ($\lambda = 1$)	99.24±0.86	92.17±4.65	67.45±10.86	27.51±11.12	6.39±4.57

Table 4: Mean ± Standard Deviation for S_w for 300-d GloVe embedding. For $\epsilon = 5, 10, 20$, the Mahalanobis mechanism has significantly higher values of mean S_w than the Laplace mechanism, where statistical significance is established by comparing the 95% confidence intervals in the form of $mean \pm 1.96 \times std/\sqrt{100}$.

to the Laplace mechanism, which demonstrates a better privacy guarantee.

5.2 Utility Experiments

In the utility experiments, we compare the Mahalanobis mechanism with the multivariate Laplace mechanism in terms of text classification performance on the two real datasets.

On the Twitter Dataset, the task is to classify whether a tweet describes a disaster event, where the benchmark FastText model (Joulin et al., 2016) achieves 0.78 accuracy, 0.78 precision, and 0.69 recall. On the SMSSpam Dataset, the task is spam classification, where the benchmark Bag-of-Words

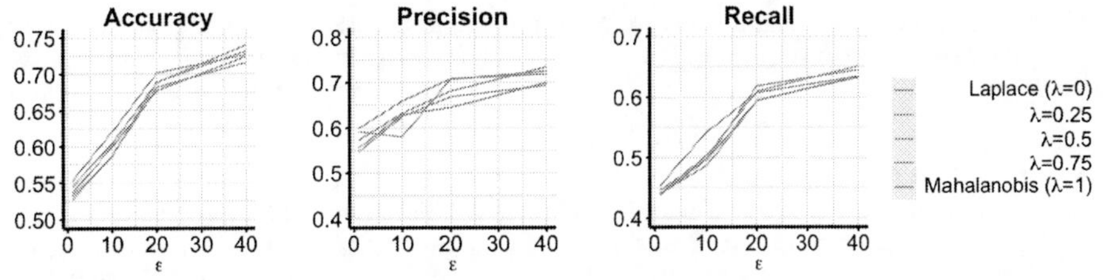

Figure 6: Text classification results on Twitter Dataset. There is no significant difference across mechanisms in terms of accuracy, precision, and recall. This shows the utility is maintained at the same level in the proposed Mahalanobis mechanism across λ.

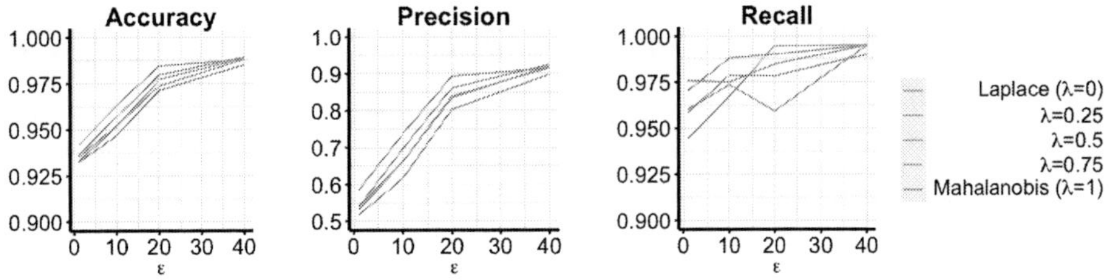

Figure 7: Text classification results on SMSSpam Dataset. There is no significant difference across mechanisms in terms of accuracy, precision, and recall. This shows the utility is maintained at the same level in the proposed Mahalanobis mechanism across λ.

model achieves 0.99 accuracy, 0.92 precision, and 0.99 recall.

In both tasks, we use 70% of the data for training, and 30% of the data for testing. The word embedding vectors are from 300-d FastText. Figure 6 and Figure 7 present the utility results in terms of accuracy, precision and recall on two text classification tasks, respectively. As a general trend in both Twitter and SMSSpam Dataset, the classification accuracy increases with ϵ and eventually approaches the benchmark performance, which is as expected. There are cases where the recall drops when ϵ increases in SMSSpam Dataset, but such drop is not significant as the recall values are all around 0.95 or higher. Across the range of λ, the difference between utility is negligible between the Mahalanobis mechanism and the multivariate Laplace mechanism. Together with results in Section 5.1, we conclude that our proposed mechanism improves the privacy statistics while maintaining the utility at the same level.

6 Conclusions

We develop a differentially private Mahalanobis mechanism for text perturbation. Compared to the existing multivariate Laplace mechanism, our mechanism exploits the geometric property of elliptical noise so as to improve the privacy statistics while maintaining a similar level of utility. Our method can be readily extended to the privacy-preserving analysis on other natural language processing tasks, where utility can be defined according to specific needs.

We remark that the choice of Σ as the global covariance matrix of the word embeddings can be generalized to the personalized covariance matrix within the neighborhood of each word. In this sense, local sensitivity can be used instead of global sensitivity to calibrate the privacy-utility tradeoff. This can be done by adding a preprocessing clustering step on the word embeddings in the vocabulary, and then perform the Mahalanobis mechanism within each cluster using the cluster-specific covariance matrix.

Furthermore, the choice of the tuning parameter λ can also be formulated as an optimization problem with respect to pre-specified privacy and utility constraints. Since λ is the only tuning parameter on a bounded interval of $[0, 1]$, a grid search would suffice, which can be conducted by finding the λ value that maximizes the utility (privacy) objective given the fixed privacy (utility) constraints.

References

Tiago A Almeida, José María G Hidalgo, and Akebo Yamakami. 2011. Contributions to the study of sms spam filtering: new collection and results. In *Proceedings of the 11th ACM symposium on Document engineering*, pages 259–262.

Balamurugan Anandan, Chris Clifton, Wei Jiang, Mummoorthy Murugesan, Pedro Pastrana-Camacho, and Luo Si. 2012. t-plausibility: Generalizing words to desensitize text. *Trans. Data Priv.*, 5(3):505–534.

Miguel E Andrés, Nicolás E Bordenabe, Konstantinos Chatzikokolakis, and Catuscia Palamidessi. 2013. Geo-indistinguishability: Differential privacy for location-based systems. In *Proceedings of the 2013 ACM SIGSAC conference on Computer & communications security*, pages 901–914.

Ghazaleh Beigi, Kai Shu, Ruocheng Guo, Suhang Wang, and Huan Liu. 2019. I am not what i write: Privacy preserving text representation learning. *arXiv preprint arXiv:1907.03189*.

Piotr Bojanowski, Edouard Grave, Armand Joulin, and Tomas Mikolov. 2017. Enriching word vectors with subword information. *Transactions of the Association for Computational Linguistics*, 5:135–146.

Konstantinos Chatzikokolakis, Miguel E Andrés, Nicolás Emilio Bordenabe, and Catuscia Palamidessi. 2013. Broadening the scope of differential privacy using metrics. In *International Symposium on Privacy Enhancing Technologies Symposium*, pages 82–102. Springer.

Konstantinos Chatzikokolakis, Catuscia Palamidessi, and Marco Stronati. 2015. Constructing elastic distinguishability metrics for location privacy. *Proceedings on Privacy Enhancing Technologies*, 2015(2):156–170.

Romain Couillet and Matthew McKay. 2014. Large dimensional analysis and optimization of robust shrinkage covariance matrix estimators. *Journal of Multivariate Analysis*, 131:99–120.

Chad Cumby and Rayid Ghani. 2011. A machine learning based system for semi-automatically redacting documents. In *Twenty-Third IAAI Conference*.

Michael J Daniels and Robert E Kass. 2001. Shrinkage estimators for covariance matrices. *Biometrics*, 57(4):1173–1184.

Roy De Maesschalck, Delphine Jouan-Rimbaud, and Désiré L Massart. 2000. The mahalanobis distance. *Chemometrics and intelligent laboratory systems*, 50(1):1–18.

Josep Domingo-Ferrer, Agusti Solanas, and Jordi Castellà-Roca. 2009. h (k)-private information retrieval from privacy-uncooperative queryable databases. *Online Information Review*.

C. Dwork, A. Smith, T. Steinke, J. Ullman, and S. Vadhan. 2015. Robust traceability from trace amounts. In *2015 IEEE 56th Annual Symposium on Foundations of Computer Science*, pages 650–669.

Cynthia Dwork. 2008. Differential privacy: A survey of results. In *International conference on theory and applications of models of computation*, pages 1–19. Springer.

Cynthia Dwork, Frank McSherry, Kobbi Nissim, and Adam Smith. 2006. Calibrating noise to sensitivity in private data analysis. In *Theory of cryptography conference*, pages 265–284. Springer.

Cynthia Dwork, Aaron Roth, et al. 2014. The algorithmic foundations of differential privacy. *Foundations and Trends in Theoretical Computer Science*, 9(3-4):211–407.

Natasha Fernandes, Mark Dras, and Annabelle McIver. 2019. Generalised differential privacy for text document processing. In *International Conference on Principles of Security and Trust*, pages 123–148. Springer, Cham.

Oluwaseyi Feyisetan, Borja Balle, Thomas Drake, and Tom Diethe. 2020. Privacy-and utility-preserving textual analysis via calibrated multivariate perturbations. In *Proceedings of the 13th International Conference on Web Search and Data Mining*, pages 178–186.

Oluwaseyi Feyisetan, Tom Diethe, and Thomas Drake. 2019. Leveraging hierarchical representations for preserving privacy and utility in text. In *2019 IEEE International Conference on Data Mining (ICDM)*, pages 210–219. IEEE.

Rob Hall, Alessandro Rinaldo, and Larry Wasserman. 2013. Differential privacy for functions and functional data. *Journal of Machine Learning Research*, 14(Feb):703–727.

Rob Hall et al. 2012. *New Statistical Applications for Differential Privacy*. Ph.D. thesis, PhD thesis, PhD thesis, Carnegie Mellon.

Steven Hill, Zhimin Zhou, Lawrence Saul, and Hovav Shacham. 2016. On the (in) effectiveness of mosaicing and blurring as tools for document redaction. *Proceedings on Privacy Enhancing Technologies*, 2016(4):403–417.

et al. Homer N, Szelinger S. 2008. Resolving individuals contributing trace amounts of dna to highly complex mixtures using high-density snp genotyping microarrays. *PLoS Genet*, 4(8)(e1000167).

Armand Joulin, Edouard Grave, Piotr Bojanowski, and Tomas Mikolov. 2016. Bag of tricks for efficient text classification. *arXiv preprint arXiv:1607.01759*.

Shiva Prasad Kasiviswanathan, Homin K Lee, Kobbi Nissim, Sofya Raskhodnikova, and Adam Smith. 2011. What can we learn privately? *SIAM Journal on Computing*, 40(3):793–826.

Prasanta Chandra Mahalanobis. 1936. On the generalised distance in statistics. *Proceedings of the National Institute of Sciences of India*, 2(1):49–55.

A. Narayanan and V. Shmatikov. 2008. Robust de-anonymization of large sparse datasets. In *2008 IEEE Symposium on Security and Privacy (sp 2008)*, pages 111–125.

Rina Okada, Kazuto Fukuchi, and Jun Sakuma. 2015. Differentially private analysis of outliers. In *Joint European Conference on Machine Learning and Knowledge Discovery in Databases*, pages 458–473. Springer.

Hwee Hwa Pang, Xuhua Ding, and Xiaokui Xiao. 2010. Embellishing text search queries to protect user privacy.

Jeffrey Pennington, Richard Socher, and Christopher D Manning. 2014. Glove: Global vectors for word representation. In *Proceedings of the 2014 conference on empirical methods in natural language processing (EMNLP)*, pages 1532–1543.

Albin Petit, Thomas Cerqueus, Sonia Ben Mokhtar, Lionel Brunie, and Harald Kosch. 2015. Peas: Private, efficient and accurate web search. In *2015 IEEE Trustcom/BigDataSE/ISPA*, volume 1, pages 571–580. IEEE.

Ahmed Salem, Yang Zhang, Mathias Humbert, Pascal Berrang, Mario Fritz, and Michael Backes. 2018. Ml-leaks: Model and data independent membership inference attacks and defenses on machine learning models. *arXiv preprint arXiv:1806.01246*.

David Sánchez and Montserrat Batet. 2016. C-sanitized: A privacy model for document redaction and sanitization. *Journal of the Association for Information Science and Technology*, 67(1):148–163.

David SáNchez, Jordi Castellà-Roca, and Alexandre Viejo. 2013. Knowledge-based scheme to create privacy-preserving but semantically-related queries for web search engines. *Information Sciences*, 218:17–30.

et al. Sankararaman S., Obozinski G. 2009. Genomic privacy and limits of individual detection in a pool. *Nat Genet*, 41:965–967.

Juliane Schäfer and Korbinian Strimmer. 2005. A shrinkage approach to large-scale covariance matrix estimation and implications for functional genomics. *Statistical applications in genetics and molecular biology*, 4(1).

R. Shokri, M. Stronati, C. Song, and V. Shmatikov. 2017. Membership inference attacks against machine learning models. In *2017 IEEE Symposium on Security and Privacy (SP)*, pages 3–18.

Latanya Sweeney. 1997. Weaving technology and policy together to maintain confidentiality. *The Journal of Law, Medicine & Ethics*, 25(2-3):98–110. PMID: 11066504.

Isabel Wagner and David Eckhoff. 2018. Technical privacy metrics: a systematic survey. *ACM Computing Surveys (CSUR)*, 51(3):1–38.

Rik Warren, Robert F Smith, and Anne K Cybenko. 2011. Use of mahalanobis distance for detecting outliers and outlier clusters in markedly non-normal data: a vehicular traffic example. Technical report, SRA INTERNATIONAL INC DAYTON OH.

Shiming Xiang, Feiping Nie, and Changshui Zhang. 2008. Learning a mahalanobis distance metric for data clustering and classification. *Pattern recognition*, 41(12):3600–3612.

Yuxiang Zhang, Bo Du, Liangpei Zhang, and Shugen Wang. 2015. A low-rank and sparse matrix decomposition-based mahalanobis distance method for hyperspectral anomaly detection. *IEEE Transactions on Geoscience and Remote Sensing*, 54(3):1376–1389.

Xuemei Zhao, Yu Li, and Quanhua Zhao. 2015. Mahalanobis distance based on fuzzy clustering algorithm for image segmentation. *Digital Signal Processing*, 43:8–16.

A Additional Information on the Twitter and SMSSpam Data

Data	Twitter	SMSSpam
Number of records	7,613	5,574
Words per record	7.3±3.0	15.6±11.4
Vocabulary size	22,213	9,515
d_{max}/d_{min}	35.28	8.92
$\overline{d}_{:50}/\overline{d}_{-50:}$	4.47	5.67
$\overline{p}_{:50}$	0.1%	0.4%

Table 5: d_{max} is the largest Euclidean distance to the nearest word embedding in the vocabulary; d_{min} is the smallest Euclidean distance to the nearest word embedding in the vocabulary; $\overline{d}_{:50}$ is the mean distance to the nearest word embedding for the top 50 words in the sparse regions (largest distance to nearest neighbors); $\overline{d}_{-50:}$ is the mean distance to the nearest word embedding for the top 50 words in the dense regions (smallest distance to nearest neighbors). These ratio statistics demonstrate the heterogeneity in the density of the word embedding space. $\overline{p}_{:50}$ is the mean percentage of records that contains the top 50 words in the sparse regions, which suggests that those words in the sparse regions are indeed rare words that can be used to link to specific records.

Identifying and Classifying Third-party Entities in Natural Language Privacy Policies

Mitra Bokaei Hosseini & *PragyanKC*
St. Mary's University / 1 Camino Santa Maria, San Antonio, TX 78228
& *IrwinReyes*
Two Six Labs, LLC / 901 N. Stuart St., Arlington, VA 22203
& *SergeEgelman*
International Computer Science Institute / 1947 Center St, Berkeley, CA 94704

Abstract

App developers often raise revenue by contracting with third party ad networks, which serve targeted ads to end-users. To this end, a free app may collect data about its users and share it with advertising companies for targeting purposes. Regulations such as General Data Protection Regulation (GDPR) require transparency with respect to the recipients (or categories of recipients) of user data. These regulations call for app developers to have privacy policies that disclose those third party recipients of user data. Privacy policies provide users transparency into what data an app will access, collect, shared, and retain. Given the size of app marketplaces, verifying compliance with such regulations is a tedious task. This paper aims to develop an automated approach to extract and categorize third party data recipients (i.e., entities) declared in privacy policies. We analyze 100 privacy policies associated with most downloaded apps in the Google Play Store. We crowdsource the collection and annotation of app privacy policies to establish the ground truth with respect to third party entities. From this, we train various models to extract third party entities automatically. Our best model achieves average F1 score of 66% when compared to crowdsourced annotations.

1 Introduction

According to statistics from Google Play Store [1] and App Store [2] there are about 2.2 and 2.8 million applications (apps) in various categories, available for download on each platform, respectively. To generate revenue from targeted advertising, apps often collect user data such as real-time location, financial information, friends list, photos, and contact information, among others. Apps inform users of this activity through privacy policies, which detail the kinds of personal data being collected, how the data is being used, and with whom the data is shared. Consumer surveys reveal that over 90% of users accept legal terms and conditions without reading them Deloitte (2017). Moreover, statistics from a younger group with ages 18 to 34, showed that more than 97% of users never read the privacy policy and were unaware of the fact that their data has been shared to various third party companies Deloitte (2017). Such challenges arise due to the following facts. First, privacy policies are too complex and long-winded McDonald and Cranor (2008), and consumers lack the bandwidth to read and comprehend each and every privacy policy for all the services they use. Second, the asymmetric power between businesses and consumers yields "take-it-or-leave-it" attitude forced by businesses Acquisti (2010), where a consumer who doesn't like the terms being offered, is likely to be dismissed because the loss will be negligible.

Recent incidents highlight the importance of user awareness concerning third-party data collection in mobile apps. In August 2020, following a lawsuit brought about by the Los Angeles City Attorney's Office, The Weather Channel agreed to give users control over how their location data would be shared [3]. The lawsuit alleged The Weather Channel app improperly shared location data with third parties, when consumers only con-

[1] play.google.com
[2] https://www.apple.com/ios/app-store/
[3] https://apnews.com/f6a83c0b8e0a65563e4c76955c37c0ab

Proceedings of the Second Workshop on Privacy in Natural Language Processing, pages 18–27
Online, Nov 20, 2020 ©2020 Association for Computational Linguistics
https://doi.org/10.18653/v1/P17

sented to using it to find local weather reports. Similarly, the US Federal Trade Commission settled with children's app developer HyperBeard Inc. for allowing advertisers to collect tracking information from young users, in violation of the Children's Online Privacy Protection Act [4].

Recent regulatory frameworks, such as General Data Protection Regulation (GDPR) and California Consumer Privacy Act (CCPA), require app development companies to be more concrete on the data recipients listed in the privacy policies and disclose the categories of third parties with whom the app may share personally identifiable data. Such third parties, include affiliates, advertising networks, and analytics providers.

Previous works have proposed machine learning models to extract categories of data practices, such as data collection, usage, and sharing statements from privacy policies Zimmeck et al. (2017); Harkous et al. (2018). These models utilize natural language processing techniques to identify relevant features for automated extraction. However, these models fail to identify and categorize third party entities in sharing data practices of mobile apps. In this paper, we aim to analyze sharing data practices in privacy policies of mobile apps to develop an automated approach to extract and categorize third party entities. The third party entities can fall into two main categories: (1) generic third party entities, such as advertisers, partners, and affiliates; and (2) specific third party entities, such as Google Analytics, Facebook, and PayPal. For this reason, we first collect privacy policies of 100 mobile apps from Spain, which were associated with 485 most downloaded apps in Google Play. We use crowdsourcing to annotate and extract the third party categories and names from these policies. These annotations are used to train and evaluate implementations of Stanford CoreNLP CRF, scikit-learn CRF, Bi-LSTM, and Bi-LSTM CRF as named entity extraction (NER) models. Through this research, we study the feasibility of automatically extracting third party entities from privacy policy text using the crowdsourced annotated data.

To summarize, the contributions of this paper are two fold: (1) empirical evaluation of a pre-trained model to extract third party entities from privacy policies; (2) training and evaluation of various models to extract and categorize third party entities using the annotated data from 100 privacy policies.

Our results indicate poor performance of the pre-trained NER model on privacy policy corpus and the importance of training NER models for domain-specific purposes. Further, our experiment results suggest that natural language features in Stanford CoreNLP CRF model provides the best performance for extracting and categorizing third party entities. This model achieves F1 scores of 79% and 53% for generic and specific third party extraction, respectively.

This paper is organized as follows. In § 2 and § 3, we discuss background and related work. In § 4 we introduce our method in text analysis of privacy policies. In § 5, we present the evaluation and results, followed by discussion, threats to validity, and concluding remarks in § 6, § 7, and § 8.

2 Background

Named Entity Recognition (NER) The first step in most natural language processing tasks is to detect and classify all the proper names mentioned in natural language text – a task generally referred to as named entity recognition (NER) Jurafsky and Martin (2008). Generic NER models tend to focus on finding the names of people, places and organizations that are mentioned in *ordinary news texts*. In this paper, we utilize three different NER models, including Conditional Random Field, Bi-LSTM, and Bi-LSTM with CRF.

Word Embedding Distributed representation of a word as a vector in some m-dimensional space that helps learning algorithms achieve better performance by grouping similar words together Mikolov et al. (2013); Bengio et al. (2003). Each vector dimension represents some feature of the words' semantics in a corpus. In this paper, we adopt Word2Vec [5], an implementation of the Skip-gram model to construct domain-specific word embeddings, which is discussed in § 4.4.

3 Related Work

Researchers have proposed methods to ensure data transparency and compliance by analyzing data

[4]https://www.ftc.gov/news-events/press-releases/2020/06/developer-apps-popular-children-agrees-settle-ftc-allegations-it

[5]https://code.google.com/archive/p/word2vec/

practices expressed in privacy policies. For example, Breaux et al. formalized data practice requirements from privacy policies using Description Logic to automatically detect conflicting requirements and to trace data flows across policies of interacting services Breaux et al. (2009, 2014). This method relies on a small set of manually annotated privacy policies to instantiate the language. Further, initial attempts in automated analysis of privacy policy text have largely focused on readability scores Massey et al. (2013); Meiselwitz (2013); Ermakova et al. (2015).

Prior to introduction of GDPR, studies have focused on identifying policy sections related to different data practices (e.g., collection, use, and sharing) using machine learning models trained on web-based apps' privacy policies Ramanath et al. (2014); Liu et al. (2018); Wilson et al. (2016); Zimmeck et al. (2017); Harkous et al. (2018). In these studies, each segment of the privacy policy is mapped to data types from a pre-defined set of keywords, including "location", "contact", or "identifier." These studies fail to automatically extract the exact data types from the segments and identify data types that don't exist in the pre-defined set. Further, approaches that map data types to a small number of broad categories introduce inaccuracies because the mapping is based on satisficing where subtle differences between the meanings of two or more types are ignored **?**. For example, the phrase "WiFi SSID" can be construed to mean a type of location information Zimmeck et al. (2017) when location is one of a few categories to choose from (i.e., the categorization fits given the constraints). However, the term actually describes a technology that must be combined with the SSID's device information (e.g., MAC address) before it can be indirectly correlated with location; it should not be directly related to location on its own.

GDPR requires the data controllers to disclose, among others, the data recipients' categories or names (while the WP29 suggests that "the default position is that a data controller should provide information on the actual (named) recipients of the personal data"). Since 2018, majority of the privacy polices introduced updates in their terms and changes to their structure to be compliant with the new regulations. Therefore, we focus on creation of a corpus containing recently published privacy policies for our analysis.

Some studies specifically focused on automatically classifying web-based privacy policy sentences into various GDPR requirements, including "opt outs" Sathyendra et al. (2017); Tesfay et al. (2018). Researchers also utilized string searching techniques to find third-party domain names in privacy policy text Libert (2018). In contrast to these studies, our goal is to automatically extract any mentions of third party entities, including generic third party names (e.g., third parties, advertisers, affiliates, analytics services) and specific third party entities (e.g., Google Analytics, Amazon Web Services, Facebook, Paypal) from mobile apps privacy policies.

4 Privacy Policy Analysis

In this section, we first discuss our approach for constructing a corpus of 100 privacy policies. This corpus is used to train and evaluate various models to extract and classify third party entities. Second, we introduce a pilot study on five privacy policies selected from the corpus. Through the pilot study, we provide evidence on why *pre-trained* named entity recognition (NER) models on news corpus, such as Stanford CoreNLP CRF [6] cannot provide desirable results. Third, we describe our crowd-sourcing approach to annotate the privacy policy corpus. Finally, we utilize the annotations toward training and evaluation of various NER models.

4.1 Privacy Policy Corpus

Our corpus of privacy policies was drawn from the "Privacy Policy" links available on Google Play Store app pages. In **June 2018**, right after the General Data Protection Regulation (GDPR) (i.e., the new privacy law for the European Union (EU)) was put into effect, we crawled the "Top Free" charts in each of the Play Store's categories to find privacy policies. We specifically targeted a European country as the location to download the privacy polices. As a result, we downloaded **100 privacy policies** associated with 485 most downloaded apps.

We used Selenium-automated headless Firefox instances to save the contents of those privacy policy links. Privacy policies were scraped by saving the HTML content of the links after they finished loading. HTML privacy policies were then pre-processed using BeautifulSoup to do a best-effort

[6] https://stanfordnlp.github.io/CoreNLP/ner.html

extraction of the policy body in plaintext. All subsequent labeling and analysis was performed on these plaintext privacy policies.

4.2 Pilot Study

Named Entity Recognition (NER) models label sequences of words in a text which are the names of things, such as person and company names. These models can be used to extract third party entities from privacy policies. For this pilot study, we utilize implementation of Conditional Random Field (CRF) model in Stanford CoreNLP. This model is trained on an annotated newswire dataset (CoNLL-2003).

To analyze if this pre-trained model can extract generic and specific third party entities from privacy policies, we randomly select five privacy policies from the privacy policy corpus. To create a gold standard on the set of five polices and identify the third party generic and specific names, we setup an annotation task on Amazon Mechanical Turk (AMT). Three privacy experts (including the first and third authors) annotated the privacy policies based on a coding frame discussed below. Finally, we compare the extracted generic and specific third party entities with the extracted results by applying pre-trained CRF model implementation in Stanford CoreNLP. Next, we discuss our annotation task setup to construct the gold standard, followed by analysis of the pilot study results.

To set up the annotation task, we first itemize selected privacy policies into paragraphs of ~120 words, yielding 151 crowd worker annotation tasks and publish the tasks as Human Intelligence Tasks (HITs) on AMT. We preserve larger spans if the statements contain an anaphoric reference to a previous sentence (e.g., "we share your information with third party entities. These entities include...") or when the statement contains subparts or bullet points that depend on the context provided by the earlier sentences.

Next, we ask annotators to annotate the itemized privacy policy segments in each HIT based on the coding frame presented in Figure 1. The coding frame for this annotation task consist of two codes: *Generic Third Parties*, which we define as "categories or types of third parties with whom the application may share information with or use their services, e.g., third-party partners, affiliates, advertisers, analytics services;" and *Specific Third Parties*, which we define as "specific names of organizations that the application may share information with or use their services, such as Google Analytics, Amazon Web Services, Facebook, Paypal." Some paragraphs do not contain any third party entities, therefore, annotators were instructed to select a text box indicating "The paragraph does not contain any third-party categories or names." Finally, we compile the annotations where **two or more annotators** agreed on. We cannot use inter-rater reliability to evaluate consensus for phrase-level coding because the non-coded words dominate coded words and annotators generally agree about which phrases not to code Breaux and Schaub (2014). Figure 2 illustrates a HIT which is annotated using the codes *Generic Third Parties* and *Specific Third Parties*.

Table 1: Pilot Study Results

Model	Precision	Recall	F1
CoreNLP CRF	0.46	0.17	0.24

Through this pilot study, experts annotated a total of 148 unique third parties, including 117 and 31 generic and specific unique third party entities, respectively. To extract third party entities using a pre-trained CRF model, we applied Stanford CoreNLP implementation of CRF on itemized segments of five privacy policies. We compared the extracted entities with the experts annotations as our gold standard. Through this comparison, we calculate precision, recall, and F1 performance measures using true positives (TPs), false positives (FPs), false negatives (FNs), and Equations 1, 2, and 3. An extracted entity is a TP, if it is annotated as either generic or specific third party by the experts, otherwise the extracted entity is a FP. If an annotated generic or specific third party cannot be found in the list of extracted entities by the pre-trained CRF model, we consider the annotation as FN. Table 1 shows precision, recall and F1 score for our pilot study.

$$precision = TP/(TP + FP) \tag{1}$$

$$recall = TP/(TP + FN) \tag{2}$$

$$F1 = 2 \times \frac{precision \times recall}{precision + recall} \tag{3}$$

Based on the results, the pre-trained NER model on the news corpus cannot be effectively used on privacy policy domain. Therefore, there is a need to acquire a privacy policy corpus that contains annotations for generic and specific third

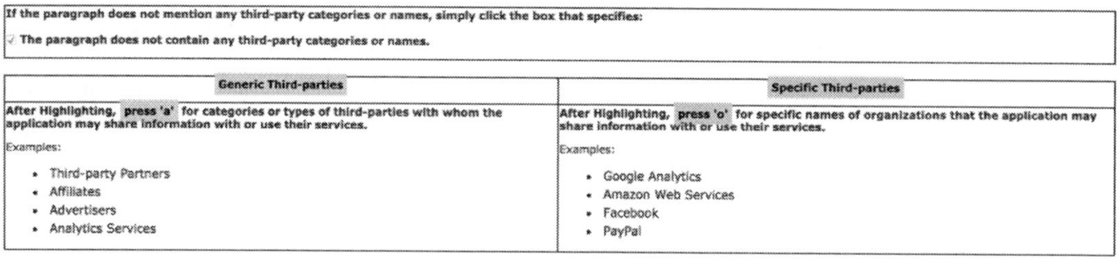

Figure 1: Third Party Annotation Coding Frame

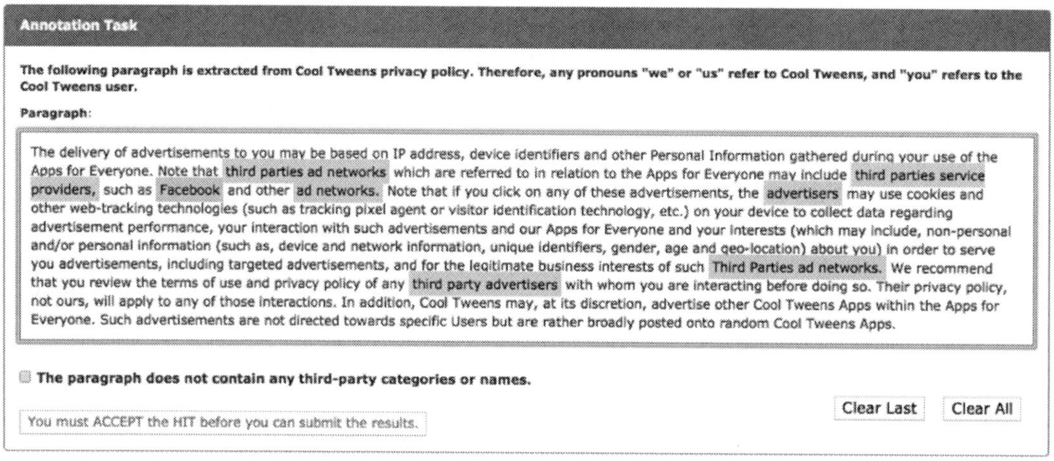

Figure 2: Annotation Example for a Privacy Policy Paragraph

party entities. This annotated corpus can be used to train various NER models. Next, we describe our efforts to construct such annotated corpus, which is then used to train and evaluate NER models.

4.3 Annotating the Corpus

We published paragraphs from 100 privacy policies on AMT and recruited workers to annotate the paragraphs based on the coding frame and instructions in Figure 1.

To recruit qualified workers for annotation, we created a qualification test on AMT. The successful workers where then granted access to annotate the privacy policies. For the qualification test, the workers were required to have HIT approval rate greater than 95 % and locate in the U.S. The qualification test HIT contains three privacy policy paragraphs that were randomly selected from the pilot study (see Section 4.2). Therefore, we had the gold standard for the annotations in the selected paragraphs. From the selected three paragraphs, one did not contain any third party entities. We used the instructions showed in Figure 1 for the qualification test. We hired 500 workers to take the qualification test. We manually analyzed the results of 500 HITs and compared the annotations with our gold standard. This analysis results in disqualifying 182 annotators due to combination of reasons, such as missing entities compared to the gold standard, marking a paragraph as not containing third parties by mistake, annotating first-party entities, annotations that spanned over English pronouns, and annotating information types.

To construct the annotated corpus, we invited all qualified workers for annotating 100 privacy polices. We follow the approach mentioned in § 4.2 to itemize the privacy policies to individual paragraphs, yielding 2,816 crowd worker annotator tasks. To achieve consensus on these tasks, each task needs to be completed by three workers. Workers are instructed to use coding frame as mentioned in Figure 1. Finally, we compile the annotations where **two or more annotators** agreed on and itemized the annotations Bhatia and Breaux (2015). The annotations resulted in 1,391 unique third party entities, including 948 generic categories and 443 specific (i.e., organization) names.

Train and Test Split Our goal is to train NER models using our annotated corpus. Therefore, we randomly split the annotated policies into training ($n = 70$) and test ($n = 30$) sets. We use the annotated policies in the training set for developing our NER models. The test set is set aside to prevent over-fitting.

4.4 Automated Named Entity Extraction

We characterize the detection and classification of third-party entities as named entity recognition (NER) problem.

Named Entity Recognition Third party entities are categorized as either (1)*generic third party*: general types of third-parties with whom an app may share information with or use their services (e.g., partners, affiliates, advertisers, etc.); or (2) *specific third party* names of organizations that the app may share information with or use their services (e.g., Google Analytics, Amazon Web Services, Facebook, etc.). To automatically extract and categorize these entities, we train various NER models, including Conditional Random Field (CRF), Bi-LSTM, and Bi-LSTM with CRF.

Preprocessing We utilize Stanford CoreNLP to tokenize sentences in the annotated privacy policy corpus. Further, we identify the part-of-speech (POS) tags for each token. As a result, each token is associated with a POS tag, an annotation tag (i.e, 'g': **generic**, 's': **specific**, 'o': **none**), and a sentence number. The preprocessed format of the privacy policy corpus is used to train and evaluate NER models as discussed below.

Vectorization (Word Embedding) Prior to training NER models using tokenized annotated corpus, we generate vector representation of each word in our corpus. For this reason, we use two methods to create vector representation for words (i.e., word embeddings): (1) Bag-of-Words (BoW); and (2) Word2Vec.

For BoW, every word in our corpus is assigned to a unique number. Sentences in the corpus are encoded with a sequence of numbers representing the words. The sequences are then passed to Bi-LSTM and Bi-LSTM CRF models that we discuss later.

To create domain-specific word embeddings, we followed the approach by Harkous et al. Harkous et al. (2018) and trained the Word2Vec model using 77,556 English privacy policies collected from mobile applications on the Google Play Store [7]. As a result, every word in our privacy corpus can be presented using 200-dimension embedding. Common-purpose word embeddings trained on the English Wikipedia dump Pennington et al. (2014); Bojanowski et al. (2017); Ling et al. (2015) or Google News dataset Mikolov et al. (2013) exist, however, previous research has shown improvements on classification accuracy by utilizing domain-specific word embeddings.

To train Word2Vec method using privacy policies, we crawled the metadata archive for more than 1,402,894 Android apps provided by the PlayDrone project Viennot et al. (2014) from which 109,933 contained a valid link to a privacy policy. We used the BeautifulSoup library in Python to extract the text from the HTML files by stripping HTML tags associated with: head, script, URL, navigation, button, and option information. Next, we filtered non-English policy text files, yielding 77,556 privacy policies with the majority of text in English by using the DetectLang library in Python. In the next step, for each privacy policy, we tokenized the sentences and removed all non-English sentences. We also expanded the contractions (e.g., "won't" is transformed to "will not"), and removed punctuation, numbers, email addresses, URLs, and special characters. Finally, we transformed the remaining characters to lower-case. The resulting pre-processed text was used to train the Word2Vec Mikolov et al. (2013) model. We utilize embedding vectors to replace the words in our privacy corpus. Therefore, a sentence is represented with a sequence of 200-dimension vectors. We use this embedding in Bi-LSTM and Bi-LSTM CRF models.

Training Using Stanford CoreNLP, scikit-learn, TensorFlow, and Keras, we train three NER models, including CRF, Bi-LSTM, and Bi-LSTM with CRF. We utilize CRF implementation from both Stanford CoreNLP [8] and scikit-learn and train these models using our training set. In addition to POS tags as a pre-extracted feature, both implementations of CRF model extract additional **natural language (NL) features**, including word parts, simplified POS tags, lower/title/upper flags, features of nearby words.

To train Bi-LSTM NER model, we implement the model using two word embedding representations. The first implementation utilizes the word

[7] http://play.google.com

[8] https://nlp.stanford.edu/software

Table 2: Performance Results

CoreNLP CRF	Prec.	Rec.	F1
Generic	0.83	0.76	**0.79**
Specific	0.60	0.47	**0.53**
scikit-learn CRF	Prec.	Rec.	F1
Generic	0.65	0.38	0.48
Specific	0.61	0.18	0.28
Bi-LSTM with BoW	Prec.	Rec.	F1
Generic	0.63	0.49	0.55
Specific	0.54	0.20	0.30
Bi-LSTM with W2V	Prec.	Rec.	F1
Generic	0.65	0.43	0.52
Specific	0.42	0.30	0.35
Bi-LSTM+CRF with BoW	Prec.	Rec.	F1
Generic	0.63	0.49	0.55
Specific	0.41	0.26	0.33
Bi-LSTM+CRF with W2V	Prec.	Rec.	F1
Generic	0.61	0.53	0.57
Specific	0.51	0.25	0.33

embeddings generated through BoW, and the second implementation incorporates word embeddings generated through Word2Vec method. Both implementations of Bi-LSTM NER are trained using our training set with 10 epochs, batch sizes of 32, and categorical cross-entropy as loss function. These parameters perform the best on the training set. As our third model, we train Bi-LSTM with CRF layer considering two implementations of the model using BoW and Word2Vec. This model utilizes an additional CRF layer for sentence sequencing on top of Bi-LSTM.

5 Evaluation and Results

We view our work as an exploration of extracting and classifying third party entities from privacy policies. As mentioned in § 4.4, we implement six NER models that utilize natural language (NL) features, Bag-of-Words (BoW), and Word2Vec (W2V). Using the train and test split of 100 privacy policies in our corpus, we train and evaluate each model. Each token in the annotated corpus is tagged with one of three labels: **generic**, **specific**, and **none**. The criteria for this selection is described in § 4.4. Table 2 shows the results of our experiments on testing set containing 30 privacy policies. Our results suggest that the implementation of CRF in Stanford CoreNLP performs the best when compared to other models and implementations. Therefore, the NL features used in Stanford CoreNLP implementation improve the NER performance. Based on these results, representing privacy policy words using domain specific context vectors learned from W2V slightly improves F1 score. However, the NL features in CRF model still outperform Bi-LSTM models that use domain specific word vector representations.

6 Discussion

We start our discussion by analyzing results from our pilot study. Through this study, we compared the experts annotations with automated third party entities extracted using a pre-trained CRF model. However, low precision, recall, and F1 score suggest poor performance of this pre-trained model for our task. The CRF model used in our pilot study was trained on news wire corpus. The tags in this pre-trained model also does not satisfy our NER task requirements. Using the pre-defined tags, we are only able to classify third party entities in privacy policies using a label called organizations (ORG) in the CRF model implementation. Therefore, for calculating performance measures in pilot study, we defined true positives (TPs) as an automatically extracted entity that is annotated as either generic or specific by our experts. Through further analysis, the pre-trained CRF model can only extract eight unique generic third party entities, and 18 unique specific third party entities.

The results from our pilot study justifies the need for training NER models using privacy policy corpus. Therefore, through this study, we construct an annotated privacy policy corpus that contains third party entities tagged with generic and specific labels. The annotations is the result of hiring qualified workers (i.e., required to successfully pass a qualification test) on AMT. Finally, the annotated corpus is used to train and test NER models. Our experiment results suggest that the natural language (NL) features used in CRF implementation of Stanford CoreNLP produces the best results when compared to our gold standard in the test set. This model considers combinations of NL features, in-

Table 3: Distribution of Tagged Tokens in Annotated Corpus

#Tokens Tagged as Generic	#Tokens Tagged as Specific	#Tokens Tagged as None	Total
9,191	2,241	422,818	434,250

cluding current word, previous word, next word, word character ngrams (up to length six), current and surrounding POS tag sequences, additional word shape features, and presence of word in left an right windows (size 4) [9] Finkel et al. (2005).

Finally, we believe the results can be improved by increasing the size of our annotated corpus. To support this claim, we present the distribution of tagged tokens in our annotated corpus in Table 3. Based on this table, our privacy policy corpus is mainly populated with non-third party tokens and is skewed toward tokens labeled with none. As another solution to this skewed annotated corpus, we foresee to apply downsampling techniques on privacy policy segments that do not contain third party entities.

7 Threats to Validity

Construct Validity Construct validity reflects whether the measurements actually measure that which they are intended to measure Yin (2017). In this paper, we provide definitions for "generic third party" and "specific third party." These definitions are reviewed by a legal expert on our team.
Internal Validity Internal validity is the extent to which a causal relationship exists between two variables or whether the investigator's inferences about the data are valid Yin (2017). In this study, we recruited laypersons to provide us with annotations for privacy policy corpus. We set a qualification task to hire qualified participants that locate in the U.S. and have HIT approval rate greater than 95%. We consider an annotation valid if at least two qualified annotators agreed on.
External Validity External validity is the extent to which findings generalize Yin (2017). The privacy policy corpus contains 100 policies associated with 485 most downloaded apps at the time. Further analysis is required to identify the categories of these apps. Moreover, further analysis is required to evaluate the performance of trained NER models on specific app domains.

[9] https://nlp.stanford.edu/nlp/javadoc/javanlp/edu/stanford/nlp/ie/NERFeatureFactory.html

8 Conclusion and Future Direction

In this paper, we aim to analyze sharing data practices of mobile apps and automatically extract and classify third party entities. For this reason, we define two categories for third party entities: (1) generic third parties, such as advertisers, partners, and affiliates; and (2) specific third party entities, including Google Analytics, Facebook, and PayPal. We first evaluate the performance of a pre-trained named entity recognition (NER) model on a set five of annotated privacy polices. The poor results of this pilot study suggest that pre-trained NER models on newswire corpus cannot be applied to extract third party entities from privacy polices. Therefore, we construct an annotated privacy policy corpus and utilize this corpus to train three different NER models. The annotated privacy policy corpus is constructed through crowdsourcing. Finally, our results shows an improvement over pilot study. Further, Stanford CoreNLP that implements CRF model using various combinations of natural language features associated with words in our corpus results in best performance when compared to the annotations.

For future, we foresee to downsample the segments of privacy polices that are not annotated as third parties. Using this strategy, we believe training and testing the Stanford CoreNLP CRF model will result in better performance. Further, regulators can utilize the results from this work to analyze the compliance of privacy policies in scale. The results of this work can also be applied to verify data practices of mobile apps. Therefore, the mobile app ecosystem can ensure a transparent environment for users.

Acknowledgments

We thank Álvaro Feal Fajardo for his participation as an expert in the pilot study. We also thank the Usable Security and Privacy Group at ICSI for their constructive feedback.

References

Alessandro Acquisti. 2010. The economics of personal data and the economics of privacy.

Yoshua Bengio, Réjean Ducharme, Pascal Vincent, and Christian Jauvin. 2003. A neural probabilistic language model. *Journal of machine learning research*, 3(Feb):1137–1155.

Jaspreet Bhatia and Travis D Breaux. 2015. Towards an information type lexicon for privacy policies. In *RELAW*, pages 19–24. IEEE.

Piotr Bojanowski, Edouard Grave, Armand Joulin, and Tomas Mikolov. 2017. Enriching word vectors with subword information. *Transactions of the Association for Computational Linguistics*, 5:135–146.

Travis D Breaux, Annie I Antón, and Eugene H Spafford. 2009. A distributed requirements management framework for legal compliance and accountability. *computers & security*, 28(1-2):8–17.

Travis D Breaux, Hanan Hibshi, and Ashwini Rao. 2014. Eddy, a formal language for specifying and analyzing data flow specifications for conflicting privacy requirements. *RE*, 19(3):281–307.

Travis D Breaux and Florian Schaub. 2014. Scaling requirements extraction to the crowd: Experiments with privacy policies. In *2014 IEEE 22nd International Requirements Engineering Conference (RE)*, pages 163–172. IEEE.

Deloitte. 2017. 2017 global mobile consumer survey: Us edition.

Tatiana Ermakova, Benjamin Fabian, and Eleonora Babina. 2015. Readability of privacy policies of healthcare websites. *Wirtschaftsinformatik*, 15.

Jenny Rose Finkel, Trond Grenager, and Christopher D Manning. 2005. Incorporating non-local information into information extraction systems by gibbs sampling. In *Proceedings of the 43rd Annual Meeting of the Association for Computational Linguistics (ACL'05)*, pages 363–370.

Hamza Harkous, Kassem Fawaz, Rémi Lebret, Florian Schaub, Kang G Shin, and Karl Aberer. 2018. Polisis: Automated analysis and presentation of privacy policies using deep learning. *arXiv preprint arXiv:1802.02561*.

Daniel Jurafsky and James H Martin. 2008. Speech and language processing: An introduction to speech recognition, computational linguistics and natural language processing. *Upper Saddle River, NJ: Prentice Hall.*

Timothy Libert. 2018. An automated approach to auditing disclosure of third-party data collection in website privacy policies. In *Proceedings of the 2018 World Wide Web Conference*, pages 207–216.

Wang Ling, Chris Dyer, Alan W Black, and Isabel Trancoso. 2015. Two/too simple adaptations of word2vec for syntax problems. In *Proceedings of the 2015 Conference of the North American Chapter of the Association for Computational Linguistics: Human Language Technologies*, pages 1299–1304.

Frederick Liu, Shomir Wilson, Peter Story, Sebastian Zimmeck, and Norman Sadeh. 2018. Towards automatic classification of privacy policy text. *School of Computer Science Carnegie Mellon University, Pittsburgh, PA, Tech. Rep. CMU-ISR-17-118R and CMULTI-17-010.*

Aaron K Massey, Jacob Eisenstein, Annie I Antón, and Peter P Swire. 2013. Automated text mining for requirements analysis of policy documents. In *2013 21st IEEE International Requirements Engineering Conference (RE)*, pages 4–13. IEEE.

Aleecia M McDonald and Lorrie Faith Cranor. 2008. The cost of reading privacy policies. *Isjlp*, 4:543.

Gabriele Meiselwitz. 2013. Readability assessment of policies and procedures of social networking sites. In *International Conference on Online Communities and Social Computing*, pages 67–75. Springer.

Tomas Mikolov, Ilya Sutskever, Kai Chen, Greg S Corrado, and Jeff Dean. 2013. Distributed representations of words and phrases and their compositionality. In *Advances in neural information processing systems*, pages 3111–3119.

Jeffrey Pennington, Richard Socher, and Christopher Manning. 2014. Glove: Global vectors for word representation. In *Proceedings of the 2014 conference on empirical methods in natural language processing (EMNLP)*, pages 1532–1543.

Rohan Ramanath, Fei Liu, Norman Sadeh, and Noah A Smith. 2014. Unsupervised alignment of privacy policies using hidden markov models. In *Proceedings of the 52nd Annual Meeting of the Association for Computational Linguistics (Volume 2: Short Papers)*, pages 605–610.

Kanthashree Mysore Sathyendra, Shomir Wilson, Florian Schaub, Sebastian Zimmeck, and Norman Sadeh. 2017. Identifying the provision of choices in privacy policy text. In *Proceedings of the 2017 Conference on Empirical Methods in Natural Language Processing*, pages 2774–2779.

Welderufael B Tesfay, Peter Hofmann, Toru Nakamura, Shinsaku Kiyomoto, and Jetzabel Serna. 2018. I read but don't agree: Privacy policy benchmarking using machine learning and the eu gdpr. In *Companion Proceedings of the The Web Conference 2018*, pages 163–166.

Nicolas Viennot, Edward Garcia, and Jason Nieh. 2014. A measurement study of google play. In *The 2014 ACM international conference on Measurement and modeling of computer systems*, pages 221–233.

Shomir Wilson, Florian Schaub, Aswarth Abhilash Dara, Frederick Liu, Sushain Cherivirala, Pedro Giovanni Leon, Mads Schaarup Andersen, Sebastian Zimmeck, Kanthashree Mysore Sathyendra, N Cameron Russell, et al. 2016. The creation and analysis of a website privacy policy corpus. In *Proceedings of the 54th Annual Meeting of the Association for Computational Linguistics (Volume 1: Long Papers)*, pages 1330–1340.

Robert K Yin. 2017. *Case study research and applications: Design and methods.* Sage publications.

Sebastian Zimmeck, Ziqi Wang, Lieyong Zou, Roger Iyengar, Bin Liu, Florian Schaub, Shomir Wilson, Norman Sadeh, Steven M. Bellovin, and Joel Reidenberg. 2017. Automated analysis of privacy requirements for mobile apps. In *NDSS*.

Surfacing Privacy Settings Using Semantic Matching

Rishabh Khandelwal, Asmit Nayak[*], Yao Yao[*] and Kassem Fawaz

University of Wisconsin–Madison

{rkhandelwal3, anayak6, yyao69, kfawaz}@wisc.edu

Abstract

Online services utilize privacy settings to provide users with control over their data. However, these privacy settings are often hard to locate, causing the user to rely on provider-chosen default values. In this work, we train privacy-settings-centric encoders and leverage them to create an interface that allows users to search for privacy settings using free-form queries. In order to achieve this goal, we create a custom Semantic Similarity dataset, which consists of real user queries covering various privacy settings. We then use this dataset to fine-tune a state of the art encoder. Using this fine-tuned encoder, we perform semantic matching between the user queries and the privacy settings to retrieve the most relevant setting. Finally, we also use the encoder to generate embeddings of privacy settings from the top 100 websites and perform unsupervised clustering to learn about the online privacy settings types. We find that the most common type of privacy settings are 'Personalization' and 'Notifications', with coverage of 35.8% and 34.4%, respectively, in our dataset.

1 Introduction

Online services provide their users with privacy settings to control information access, collection, processing, and sharing. These settings include, but are not limited to, the option to opt-out of data collection, manage notifications, and marketing emails. However, recent work [6] shows that privacy settings are often hard to locate for an average user. Even when the privacy settings pages are easily accessible, they contain numerous settings that are usually distributed over several URLs, making it challenging to find the settings of interest. For example, Facebook contains 60 privacy settings located on several different URLs. Further, several service providers expose similar settings to the user. It is desirable for the user to apply the same preference to these settings at once, instead of locating and setting their preferences at each domain.

The current privacy settings ecosystem prevents the users from making informed choices for the privacy settings; users unknowingly accept the default options for privacy settings, which tend to favor the interests of the web services over those of the users [19, 22]. Due to their non-standard nature, privacy settings have received little attention in the privacy literature than the more standard opt-out options [7, 30, 13] and privacy policies [8].

There is a need to make privacy settings to be more accessible so that users can exercise more informed choices. Achieving this objective requires crawling the websites for privacy control pages, parsing their HTML to extract the privacy settings, and presenting these settings in a more usable manner. In this paper, we tackle the latter problem of presenting privacy settings to the user by investigating the feasibility of an intra- and inter- domain search interface for privacy settings. In particular, we create a privacy setting-centric encoder and leverage it to answer the following questions:

- *Given privacy settings pages, can we build an interface to allow users to search for privacy settings accurately?*
- *Can we utilize NLP techniques to learn about the landscape of online privacy settings?*

To answer these questions, we first create a custom Semantic Similarity dataset consisting of real user queries covering various privacy settings. We use this dataset to fine-tune the Universal Sentence encoder [2] to match user queries with the

[*]Equal Contribution

Proceedings of the Second Workshop on Privacy in Natural Language Processing, pages 28–38
Online, Nov 20, 2020 ©2020 Association for Computational Linguistics
https://doi.org/10.18653/v1/P17

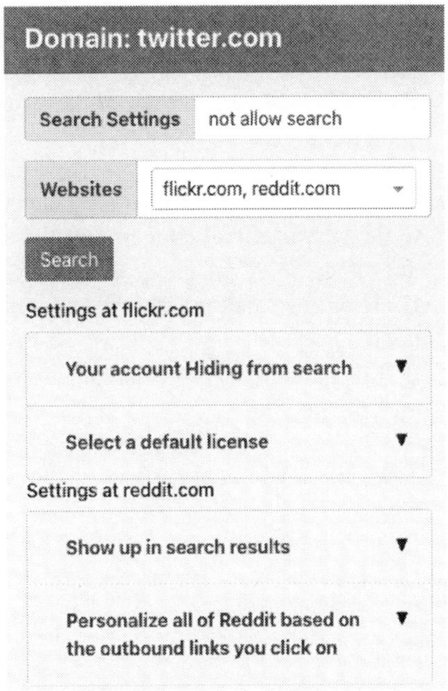

Figure 1: Example of searching across domains

settings text. Next, we represent a privacy settings page as an abstract data structure consisting of privacy groups. We manually extract the text for these privacy groups for the top 100 websites. We demonstrate the feasibility of developing an accurate intra- and inter- domain search interface for privacy settings. Finally, we leverage the developed encoder to analyze the landscape of privacy settings across different websites.

To summarize, we make the following contributions in this paper:

- We provide a manually curated Sentence Similarity Dataset of free-form user queries for privacy settings. Further, we train a privacy-setting-centric sentence encoder using this dataset.
- We develop a browser extension that uses a fine-tuned sentence encoder to enable users to search for settings in the same domain and across domains. We also evaluate the encoder using real-world queries.
- Finally, we leverage the privacy settings' embeddings to analyze the top 100 websites' privacy settings using unsupervised clustering to understand the landscape of privacy settings for popular websites.

2 Related Work

While the existing literature on understanding the landscape of privacy settings is scarce, there has been some work done in the extraction and automation of privacy settings, particularly in mobile apps' context [17, 16, 15]. Chen et al. [3] conducted a large-scale study on the usability of privacy settings for Android applications. Their methodology leverages the semantic relationship between the text descriptions of UI elements and the titles of application views to discover privacy menus hidden in apps. Liu et al. [17] studied the feasibility of generalized privacy profiles, predicting user permission decisions by modeling it as a classification problem. Jialiu et al. [15] similarly studied privacy profiles using unsupervised clustering of user preferences and app permissions. Relatedly, a new privacy application called Jumbo [27] allows users to select one of three available privacy profiles and after that sets the user's privacy settings for their set of supported mobile apps. These works are specific to Android and do not provide insights into the type of privacy settings employed by the services.

In the web domain, Nisal el al. [24] created a browser extension built on top of a previously proposed automated-extraction methodology [30] to capture opt-out choices from a website's privacy policy. The extension developed by Nisal et al. displays the extracted information to users and helps the users to enforce their opt-out settings.

In the privacy domain, prior works have used NLP techniques primarily to understand and analyze privacy policies [8, 25, 23, 1]. In particular, Harkous et al. [8] used a hierarchical text classification system to annotate segments from the privacy policy automatically. They also developed a free-form QA system for queries on privacy policies. Similarly, Oltramari et al. [25] developed PrivOnto, which analyzes privacy policies based on an ontology that uses a semantic framework to represent annotated policies; Nejad et al. [23] used text mining and rule-based semantic technologies for information extraction from contractual agreements. Andow et al. [1] proposed PolicyLint which leverages sentence level NLP techniques to identify internal contradictions within policy by capturing both positive and negative statements of data collection and sharing. There has also been some research done in using NLP for verification of compliance [33, 32] of privacy practices by smartphone apps by comparing the permissions to the privacy policy text. All these works are essentially focused on privacy policies whereas, in this work, we fine-tune the state-of-the-art sentence encoders to create privacy-setting-centric embeddings.

3 Datasets

In this section, we describe the two datasets that we created for fine-tuning the Universal Sentence Encoder and evaluating semantic matching of the natural language interpreter present in the browser extension.

3.1 Semantic Similarity Dataset

In order to fine-tune the sentence encoders, we created a custom Sentence Similarity Dataset for privacy settings, which consists of real user queries posted on Reddit. These queries are derived from the threads that ask for privacy settings related questions for the top 100[1] domains. This dataset aims to capture semantic relations between a user query and the privacy setting text.

To extract the queries, we followed a methodology similar to that of Harkous et al [8]. In particular, we searched for "privacy setting" and "notification setting" to search the subreddits of each domain from the top 100 domains. To filter out unrelated threads, we keep the ones that are posted as questions by checking for the question mark in the title of the thread. In order to refine our search such that user questions that do not contain question marks are not simply discarded, we also used two classifiers, a Multinomial Naive Bayes classifier [21], and the Stanford NLP package [21].

Using the above process, we collected 596 candidate queries automatically. Next, two of the authors manually analyzed the candidate queries with the following objectives: a) Filter out the queries if it is not related to privacy settings; b) For the remaining queries, find the corresponding setting that resolves the query and c) assign a similarity score between each pair of query and the setting. The assignment of similarity score is done according to the following rules:

- **Score 0 :** The setting and the query are completely unrelated. Example :
  Q : How to get profile edits to show up publicly?
  S : Display media that may contain sensitive content
- **Score 0.5 :** The setting and the query refer to the same general concept but the setting does not resolve the query. Example:
  Q : How to fix issues with comment notifications?
  S : Mentions Notify me when others mention my channel
- **Score 1 :** The query refers to the setting; e.g.
  Q : Comments - No notifications from replies?
  S : Replies to my comments Notify me about replies to my comments

The annotators had an overlapping set of 150 queries to measure the inter-annotator agreement. We observe that they showed high agreement on manual tagging of this set. In particular, they had a high value for Cohen's Kappa ($\kappa = 0.84$) [14]. The queries that the annotators disagreed on were resolved after further discussion. At the end of this process, we have the Sentence Similarity Dataset with a total of 596 query-setting pair consisting of 219 pairs with score 1, 150 pairs with score 0.5, and 227 pairs with score 0.

3.2 Evaluation Dataset

To evaluate the natural language interpreter backed by semantic matching in the browser extension, we created another dataset similar to Semantic Similarity Dataset. The key goals of this dataset are: a) privacy setting queries are free-form, b) each query has a corresponding setting for it. Essentially, this set is an independent set of query-setting pair with a similarity score of 1. To create such a dataset, we followed the same procedure as described in the section above, but only kept the queries for which we could find a corresponding settings option. The final outcome of this process is a set of 110 query-setting pairs covering 20 popular domains including Twitter, Reddit, Amazon etc. It is important to note that the two datasets described in this section have no overlapping queries - the first one is used for fine-tuning the encoders while the second one is used to evaluate the browser extension's semantic

[1]According to top sites ranking by Tranco: `https://tranco-list.eu/`

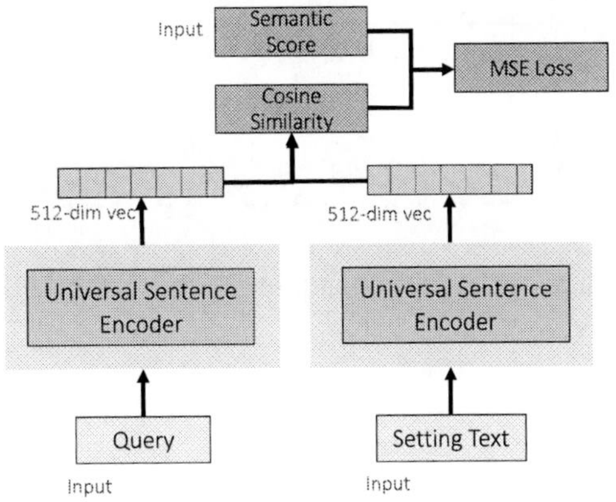

Figure 2: Schematic showing the training procedure for semantic similarity task which is used to fine-tune the Universtal Sentence Encoder

search which is built on top of the fine-tuned encoders. We also note that the Reddit queries might be structurally different than the actual queries. In particular, Reddit queries can be more descriptive whereas the actual queries are generally limited to phrases or keywords. However, since the semantic content is similar (privacy settings), we expect the encoder to perform well in both scenarios.

3.3 Takeaway

The key takeaway here is the semantic similarity dataset consisting of user-queries and privacy settings pairs. This dataset can be utilized to generate privacy-centric embeddings which can then be used to build more privacy-enhancing applications.

4 Fine Tuning the Encoder

Transfer learning has proven to be very effective in several NLP tasks [10, 4, 31, 18]. The key idea is to pre-train general embeddings on large text corpora using an unsupervised loss and then use transfer learning for downstream tasks like text classification, semantic matching, sentiment analysis, etc. The intuition behind this is inspired by the fact that humans do not learn everything from scratch, but extend learned knowledge to new domains. There are two standard techniques used for transfer learning in NLP: fine-tuning and feature-based transfer learning. In feature-based transfer learning, the main idea is to find good feature representation to minimize domain divergence and classification error [26]. In fine-tuning, the pre-trained embeddings are re-trained on downstream tasks (classification, etc.) using labeled data. Further, prior work has shown that fine-tuning achieves better performance than feature-based transfer learning [10]

In this paper, our goal is to generate privacy-settings-centric embeddings for semantic matching to enable users to search for privacy settings. Further, using these embeddings, we can understand the landscape of privacy settings by using unsupervised clustering techniques. To achieve this, we utilize the Semantic Similarity Dataset that we collected (Sec. 3.1). In particular, we fine-tune Universal Sentence Encoder (USE) [2] using the sentence similarity task with the dataset described in Sec. 3.1. USE is trained with a Deep Averaging Network. [11] and is considered as one of the state of the art sentence encoders [2]. We further note that we did not perform any pre-processing on the text as USE is designed to work with the raw textual data.

Finally, we set aside 100 query-setting pairs from the dataset for testing and we train on the remaining 496 query-setting pairs. The schematic of the training procedure is shown in Fig. 2. During training, we first pass the query and the setting text through the networks to get the embedding vectors; then we compute the cosine similarity score using the two vectors. Finally, this score and the manually annotated score are used to compute the Mean Squared Error (MSE) loss. We used Adam [12] optimizer to optimize the loss function and update the weights. We used the test set loss to decide how many iterations the training should go on for. We found that the test set loss was minimized with 10 iterations.

4.1 Evaluation of the Encoder

Next, we evaluate the encoders and the semantic search feature of the browser extension using the evaluation dataset described in Sec. 3.2. This dataset consists of 110 queries from 20 popular domains. For a baseline comparison, we evaluate the performance of semantic matching using the Universal Sentence Encoder (USE) [2] without fine-tuning. We further include two other encoders, based on SBERT [28] and SRoBERTa [28], which are retrained versions of BERT [5] and RoBERTa [20] using siamese and triplet network structures. These models are first pre-trained on Natural Language Inference (NLI) datasets and

Model	Top-1	Top-3	Top-5	Top-7
USE	63.7	84.6	92.6	97.4
SBERT-nli-stsb-base	49.2	74.3	83.4	93.6
SRoBERTa-nli-stsb-base	48.9	72.6	84.2	92.4
USE Fine-tuned	72.9	92.4	98.8	100

Table 1: Top-k accuracy in % for the different encoders in semantic matching on the Evaluation Dataset

then fine-tuned on the Semantic Textual Similarity dataset (STSB).

The evaluation results are compared in Table 1. The results show that the base model of Universal Sentence Encoder outperforms the other encoders in this task. Further, we find that the fine-tuned encoder performs better than all the other encoders tested. In particular, the results show that the user query is answered by the top-3 results 92% of the time on a given domain. Even if the relevant setting is not found in the top 3 results, the user is almost certain to find the relevant group in the top 7 results. This is particularly useful for websites like Facebook, where the number of extracted groups is more than 60. These results further show that the NLP techniques can play an important role in reducing the user's burden, particularly in making it easier to find the relevant privacy settings.

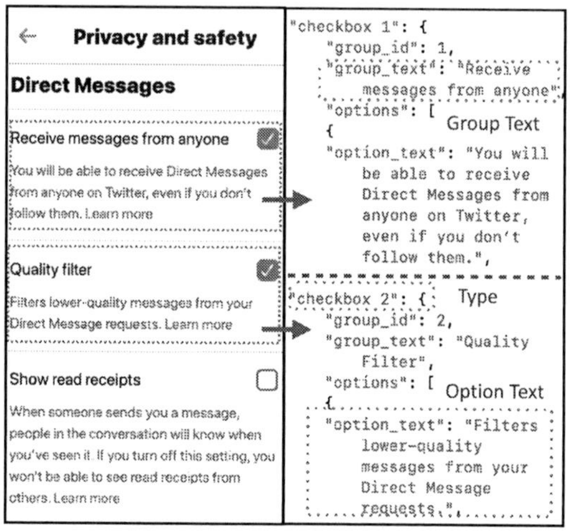

Figure 3: (Left) Example of a privacy settings page on Twitter. (Right) The abstraction of this page showing the, group texts, option texts and the type of setting. This abstraction is used to represent the privacy control pages for all the domains in our set.

We further analyze the queries and find that the length of the query has an observable effect on semantic matching. In particular, we find that as the length increases (or multiple contexts are present), the performance of semantic matching decreases. For example, consider this user query on Reddit: *"anyone know if there is a way to stop replies on tweets appearing from people you follow to accounts you do not or floods of tweets from people you do not follow but others do"*. This query concerns with replies on the tweets, but is not matched with *"Push Notifications Mentions and Replies"*. However, if we remove the second half of the query (*"from people you follow to accounts you do not or floods of tweets from people you do not follow but others do"*), then the matching is accurate. We hypothesize that the reason for this behavior is that in such cases, the extra information dilutes the the context which results in poor matching.

4.2 Takeaway

In this section, we demonstrate the use of the Semantic similarity dataset by fine-tuning the Universal Sentence Encoder to generate privacy setting centric embeddings. We further evaluate the fine-tuned encoder with real user-queries and show that it outperforms the other state-of-the-art encoders.

5 The Browser Extension

This section describes the browser extension which leverages the fine-tuned encoder to allow the user to search for privacy settings across multiple domains. We, first, start with a brief introduction of our collection method for privacy settings. We, then, describe the browser extension.

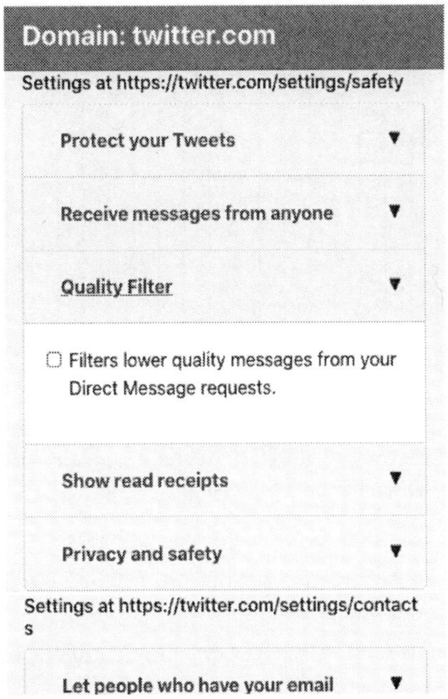

Figure 4: Displays all available settings on twitter.com in accordance with the recipe in Figure 3

Privacy Settings Extraction

In order to allow the extension to perform semantic searches, we need to extract the privacy settings text. Starting with the list of top 100 websites, we visit each domain, go to the privacy settings page, and manually extract the relevant setting text. To represent the privacy control page, we propose an abstraction of the privacy settings page as a set of privacy control groups. The control group is defined as a set of all the individual options. For example, in Fig. 3, the left panel shows the privacy settings page for Twitter. In this figure, there are three control groups, each having one option. This way, each setting option is represented as part of a group with the following attributes: (a) Group Text: text providing context for the entire group, (b) Option Text: text providing context for the option, (c) Type of setting (*radio*, *checkbox*, etc). For example, Fig. 3 shows the representation of the settings page for Twitter. During this process, we extracted privacy settings text for 67 domains. The rest of the domains either did not have privacy control pages or were not in English.

Browser Extension

We implemented the user interface in the form of a Chrome browser extension supported by a natural language query interpreter. The interpreter allows the users to search for privacy settings. The extension is backed with a back-end server where the semantic matching occurs to find the appropriate setting for the user query. The client-side is responsible for handling user interactions as well as displaying the query results from the server.

Once activated by clicking on the icon, the extension renders a basic list interface that shows the privacy settings groups for the given domain. These settings are categorized by the control URLs for that particular domain, as shown in Fig. 4. To change any setting, the user needs to click on the setting text, which opens up the privacy setting URL in a new tab where the user can choose their preferences.

The search interface of the extension allows the users to search for their setting of interest with free-form queries, as shown in Fig. 1. By default, the extension only searches for the currently active website. The user can choose to include other websites they prefer to search from a list of available websites. For example, Fig. 1 shows the search results for the query 'not allow search' for *flickr.com* and *reddit.com*. In this example, the user started from *twitter.com* but then restricted the search list to *flickr.com* and *reddit.com*. The semantic search returns the top two matches for the query. From here, the user can again click on the setting text to navigate to the privacy control page and change their preference.

Thus, the users can now search for privacy settings with free-form queries, which addresses the reachability issues of the privacy settings. Simultaneously, it also reduces the time and effort that would otherwise be needed for the user to look for privacy settings.

5.1 Takeaway

In this section, we present a browser extension that leverages semantic matching using the fine-tuned encoder to enable the users to search for privacy settings. Combined with the high top-3 accuracy of the encoder, the extension addresses the reachability issues of privacy settings and reduces the user effort in locating the settings.

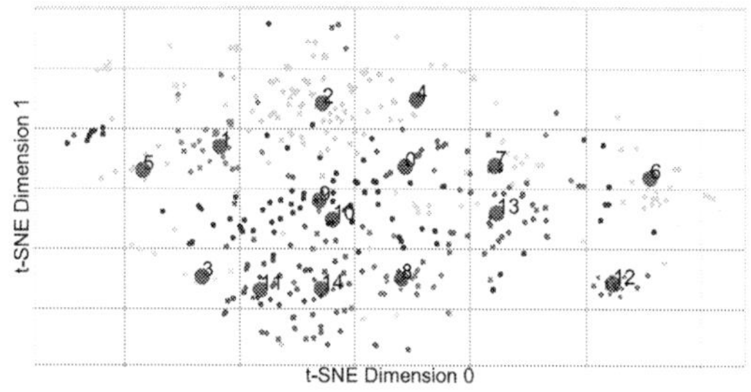

Figure 5: A 2D plot created by applying t-SNE on the multidimensional dataset containing the embeddings of the settings texts, along with the cluster centers from K-Means

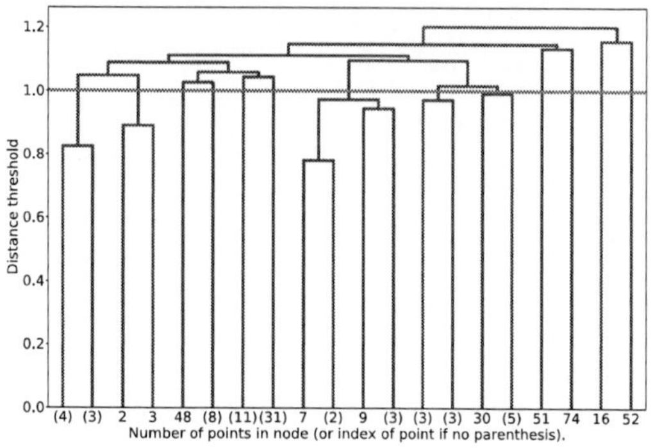

Figure 6: A dendogram showing the hierarchical tree formed from the dataset. The red line is the threshold after which the clustering stops

6 Analysis of Privacy Settings

To further understand the types of privacy settings employed by the web services, we take the privacy settings text that we extracted (Sec. 3.1), encode them using the fine-tuned encoder described in Sec. 4, and group them using unsupervised clustering. We use two types of clustering techniques; K-Means [9] and Agglomerative Hierarchical clustering [29] to perform the clustering. We further compare the results from the two techniques and find that Agglomerative Hierarchical clustering performs significantly better than K-Means clustering.

K-Means Clustering In K-Means clustering, the dataset is broken into 'k'-partitions by initially assigning k-random cluster centers, called centroids. Based on proximity to these clusters, each point in the dataset is assigned one of these random centroids. Finding the mid-point of these centers gives us new centroids and the process is repeated until the new centroid coincides with the previous ones.

To select the optimum value of k in K-Means, we manually analyze the clusters with $k = 5$, 7, 10, 13, 15, 17, and 20. We found that 13 and 15 clusters produced the best results. However, there were certain discrepancies in these clustering. For example, some of the clusters focused on narrow topics like 'Email Notifications' while other clusters contained settings from more than one topic like 'Personalizations' and 'Ads'. Furthermore, the random initial clustering employed by K-means resulted in a number of initial misclassifications of the settings.

Agglomerative Hierarchical Clustering In Agglomerative clustering, each data point is initially a cluster of its own. Then, through repeated iterations, the clusters that are the closest to each other are merged until we get one single cluster with all the data points. The above method creates a tree, as shown in Fig. 6, with the root node containing all the data points. The clusters are obtained from this tree by deciding a threshold, after which the merging stops. We used the maximum Euclidean distance between similar settings as the distance threshold for clustering sentences, which was about 1 unit. Using this, we found a total of 15 clusters with 9 main clusters and 6 outliers. The outliers in clustering can be attributed to their sentence structure and size, which diluted the embeddings.

To manually compare the two clustering techniques, two of the authors independently annotate the clusters generated by K-Means and Agglomerative clustering and concluded that the Agglomerative clustering was more accurate and coherent. They further compare their annotations and obtain high agreement with Cohen's Kappa ($\kappa = 0.87$). We attribute the reason for better performance of Agglomerative clustering to its nature, where the number of clusters is not fixed and a distance threshold is used above which clusters will not be merged. Moreover, the cluster centers of K-Means are randomly assigned. As a result, it is possible that due to the position of the initial cluster center, informative and distinct clusters are not formed. Whereas in Agglomerative clustering, each sentence/setting text is an individual cluster initially, and then these clusters are merged as long as the distance between these clusters is less than equal to the distance threshold.

Since Agglomerative clustering is the better performing method in this context, we used it to

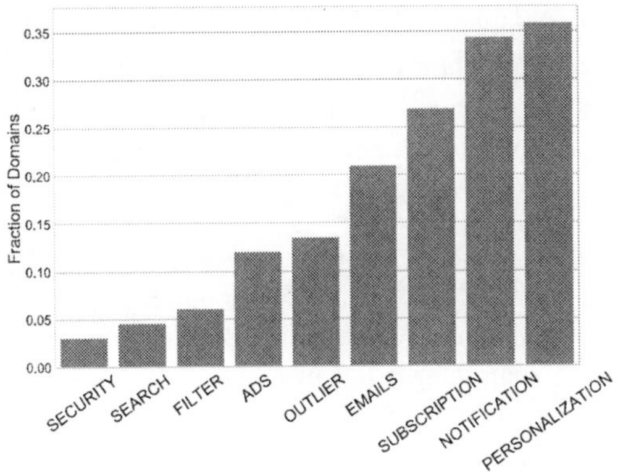

Figure 7: Coverage of the domains for the categories found using unsupervised clustering. We note that Personalization and Notification are the most common type of privacy settings employed by the web services.

cluster all the settings in our database. The main categories we found are: Notification, Emails, Subscriptions, Personalization, Ads, Security, Filter, and Search. Apart from these categories, we also notice a few outlier clusters which represent the specific features of some websites. For example, we observe a cluster with settings enabling contacts management from `twitter.com` and `alibaba.com`.

The coverage of the domains in our set for the categories found above is shown in Fig. 7. We observe that settings corresponding to Personalization and Notifications have the highest coverage. The Personalization category here includes settings directly related to the privacy of the user. For example, limiting the audience for posts for Facebook or allowing people to share images on Instagram. Other categories like Emails and Subscriptions are also covered fairly regularly. These include marketing emails and emails regarding the account - like pull request emails for Github, respectively.

Search and Filter category are examples of website-specific categories: Search includes the settings about the search engine (Bing, Google, Duckduckgo), while Filter includes settings related to quality filters from Google, Twitter, Flickr, and Bing.

We further observe that Security settings, which primarily consist of multi-factor authentication settings, are covered less. This behaviour is not surprising as multi-factor authentication is a new concept and websites are slowly starting to incorporate it. However, the trend observed in the coverage of domain showcases the lack of privacy settings provided by the websites. For example, even in the top-100 websites, only 36% provide the users with Personalization settings.

It is important to note here that the analysis done is highly dependent on the small dataset that we have; it is very likely that we missed several types of settings. For example, cookie settings that allow the user to disable ad tracking are missing. The analysis presented here however does shed light on the common privacy settings like Notification, Subscription and Personalization.

6.1 Takeaway

In this section, we provide another use case of the privacy-centric encoder. We generate the embeddings for privacy setting text of the top 100 websites and use unsupervised clustering to learn about the type of settings used by the websites. We find that there are 7 main categories with notification and personalization settings being the most common ones.

7 Limitations

In this section, we describe the technical limitations of this project.

Scaling The privacy setting text used in the analyses is extracted manually. This approach does not scale very well and is used in this work primarily to show the applicability of privacy-settings-centric encoder. It is however possible to scale the technique by developing web scraping techniques, which is left for future work. Further, scaling the analysis in Sec. 6 using hierarchical clustering to larger datasets is also a limitation as this clustering technique's complexity is quadratic with the number of data points.

Impact on Users While the extension that we propose makes it easy for the users to find privacy settings, the impact and usability of the extension are not studied in this work. In particular, studies exploring the impact of the extension on user choices are considered out of scope and are left as future work.

Completeness The analysis conducted in Sec. 6 with privacy settings is not exhaustive. The goal here is to show applications of privacy-settings-centric encoders; hence, the analysis is treated as a proof of concept analysis. In particular, we only considered first-party privacy settings, however, some websites outsource their privacy (cookies) settings to third parties. Such settings are not considered here, as a result, some type of settings might have been missed. We accept this as a limitation of this work.

8 Conclusion

In this paper, we present a Sentence Similarity Dataset for privacy settings consisting of real-world user queries about privacy settings and their corresponding settings from several domains. We further use this dataset to fine-tune Universal Sentence Encoder to generate privacy settings centric sentence encoder. To demonstrate the use case of these embeddings, we develop a browser extension that allows the users to search for their privacy settings for popular websites, including Google, Facebook, Twitter, etc. The extension is backed by a natural language interpreter that takes in the user query and performs semantic matching with the privacy settings text. Additionally, we also use the embeddings of privacy settings text to understand the type of privacy settings employed by the website by using unsupervised clustering to find that notification and personalization settings are the most common settings.

Acknowledgement

We would like to thank the anonymous reviewers for their useful comments. The work reported in this paper was supported in part by the NSF under grants 1838733, 1942014, and 2003129.

Availability

The datasets collected in this paper will be made available at `https://github.com/wi-pi/surface_privacy_data`. We also plan to make the source code public and release the plugin.

References

[1] Benjamin Andow, Samin Yaseer Mahmud, Wenyu Wang, Justin Whitaker, William Enck, Bradley Reaves, Kapil Singh, and Tao Xie. Policylint: investigating internal privacy policy contradictions on google play. In *28th USENIX Security Symposium (USENIX Security 19)*, pages 585–602, 2019.

[2] Daniel Cer, Yinfei Yang, Sheng-yi Kong, Nan Hua, Nicole Limtiaco, Rhomni St John, Noah Constant, Mario Guajardo-Cespedes, Steve Yuan, Chris Tar, et al. Universal sentence encoder. *arXiv preprint arXiv:1803.11175*, 2018.

[3] Yi Chen, Mingming Zha, Nan Zhang, Dandan Xu, Qianqian Zhao, Xuan Feng, Kan Yuan, Fnu Suya, Yuan Tian, Kai Chen, et al. Demystifying hidden privacy settings in mobile apps. In *2019 IEEE Symposium on Security and Privacy (SP)*, pages 570–586. IEEE, 2019.

[4] Andrew M Dai and Quoc V Le. Semi-supervised sequence learning. In *Advances in neural information processing systems*, pages 3079–3087, 2015.

[5] Jacob Devlin, Ming-Wei Chang, Kenton Lee, and Kristina Toutanova. Bert: Pre-training of deep bidirectional transformers for language understanding. *arXiv preprint arXiv:1810.04805*, 2018.

[6] Hana Habib, Sarah Pearman, Jiamin Wang, Yixin Zou, Alessandro Acquisti, Lorrie Faith Cranor, Norman Sadeh, and Florian Schaub. "it's a scavenger hunt": Usability of websites' opt-out and data deletion choices. In *Proceedings of the 2020 CHI Conference on Human Factors in Computing Systems*, pages 1–12, 2020.

[7] Hana Habib, Yixin Zou, Aditi Jannu, Neha Sridhar, Chelse Swoopes, Alessandro Acquisti, Lorrie Faith Cranor, Norman Sadeh, and Florian Schaub. An empirical analysis of data deletion and opt-out choices on 150 websites. In *Fifteenth Symposium on Usable Privacy and Security (SOUPS 2019)*, 2019.

[8] H Harkous, K Fawaz, R Lebret, F Schaub, KG Shin, and K Aberer. Polisis: Automated analysis and presentation of privacy policies using deep learning. In *27th USENIX Security Symposium (USENIX Security 18)*. USENIX Association, 2018.

[9] John A Hartigan and Manchek A Wong. Algorithm as 136: A k-means clustering algorithm. *Journal of the royal statistical society. series c (applied statistics)*, 28(1):100–108, 1979.

[10] Jeremy Howard and Sebastian Ruder. Universal language model fine-tuning for text classification. *arXiv preprint arXiv:1801.06146*, 2018.

[11] Mohit Iyyer, Varun Manjunatha, Jordan Boyd-Graber, and Hal Daumé III. Deep unordered composition rivals syntactic methods for text classification. In *Proceedings of the 53rd Annual Meeting of the Association for Computational Linguistics and the 7th International Joint Conference on Natural Language Processing (Volume 1: Long Papers)*, volume 1, pages 1681–1691, 2015.

[12] Diederik P Kingma and Jimmy Ba. Adam: A method for stochastic optimization. *arXiv preprint arXiv:1412.6980*, 2014.

[13] Vinayshekhar Bannihatti Kumar, Roger Iyengar, Namita Nisal, Yuanyuan Feng, Hana Habib, Peter Story, Sushain Cherivirala, Margaret Hagan, Lorrie Faith Cranor, Shomir Wilson, et al. Finding a choice in a haystack: Automatic extraction of opt-out statements from privacy policy text. In *The Web Conference (the Web Conf)*, 2020.

[14] J Richard Landis and Gary G Koch. The measurement of observer agreement for categorical data. *biometrics*, pages 159–174, 1977.

[15] Jialiu Lin, Bin Liu, Norman Sadeh, and Jason I Hong. Modeling users' mobile app privacy preferences: Restoring usability in a sea of permission settings. In *10th Symposium On Usable Privacy and Security (SOUPS 2014)*, pages 199–212, 2014.

[16] Bin Liu, Mads Schaarup Andersen, Florian Schaub, Hazim Almuhimedi, Shikun Aerin Zhang, Norman Sadeh, Yuvraj Agarwal, and Alessandro Acquisti. Follow my recommendations: A personalized privacy assistant for mobile app permissions. In *Twelfth Symposium on Usable Privacy and Security (SOUPS 2016)*, pages 27–41, 2016.

[17] Bin Liu, Jialiu Lin, and Norman Sadeh. Reconciling mobile app privacy and usability on smartphones: Could user privacy profiles help? In *Proceedings of the 23rd international conference on World wide web*, pages 201–212, 2014.

[18] Nelson F Liu, Matt Gardner, Yonatan Belinkov, Matthew E Peters, and Noah A Smith. Linguistic knowledge and transferability of contextual representations. *arXiv preprint arXiv:1903.08855*, 2019.

[19] Yabing Liu, Krishna P Gummadi, Balachander Krishnamurthy, and Alan Mislove. Analyzing facebook privacy settings: user expectations vs. reality. In *Proceedings of the 2011 ACM SIGCOMM Conference on Internet Measurement*, pages 61–70. ACM, 2011.

[20] Yinhan Liu, Myle Ott, Naman Goyal, Jingfei Du, Mandar Joshi, Danqi Chen, Omer Levy, Mike Lewis, Luke Zettlemoyer, and Veselin Stoyanov. Roberta: A robustly optimized bert pretraining approach. *arXiv preprint arXiv:1907.11692*, 2019.

[21] Kartik Nagre. nlp-question-detection. `https://github.com/kartikn27/nlp-question-detection`, 2019.

[22] Kaweh Djafari Naini, Ismail Sengor Altingovde, Ricardo Kawase, Eelco Herder, and Claudia Niederée. Analyzing and predicting privacy settings in the social web. In *International Conference on User Modeling, Adaptation, and Personalization*, pages 104–117. Springer, 2015.

[23] Najmeh Mousavi Nejad. Semantic analysis of contractual agreements to support end-user interpretation. In *EKAW (Doctoral Consortium)*, 2018.

[24] Namita Nisal, Florian Schaub, Sushain K. Cherivirala, Shomir Wilson, Kanthashree M. Sathyendra, Lorrie Faith Cranor, Margaret Hagan, and Norman Sadeh. Increasing the salience of data use opt-outs online. In *Symposium on Usable Privacy and Security 2017)*, 2017.

[25] Alessandro Oltramari, Dhivya Piraviperumal, Florian Schaub, Shomir Wilson, Sushain Cherivirala, Thomas B Norton, N Cameron Russell, Peter Story, Joel Reidenberg, and

Norman Sadeh. Privonto: A semantic framework for the analysis of privacy policies. *Semantic Web*, 9(2):185–203, 2018.

[26] Sinno Jialin Pan and Qiang Yang. A survey on transfer learning. *IEEE Transactions on knowledge and data engineering*, 22(10):1345–1359, 2009.

[27] Jumbo Privacy. Jumbo. `https://www.jumboprivacy.com/`, 2019.

[28] Nils Reimers and Iryna Gurevych. Sentence-bert: Sentence embeddings using siamese bert-networks. *arXiv preprint arXiv:1908.10084*, 2019.

[29] K Sasirekha and P Baby. Agglomerative hierarchical clustering algorithm-a. *International Journal of Scientific and Research Publications*, 83:83, 2013.

[30] Kanthashree Mysore Sathyendra, Shomir Wilson, Florian Schaub, Sebastian Zimmeck, and Norman Sadeh. Identifying the provision of choices in privacy policy text. In *Proceedings of the 2017 Conference on Empirical Methods in Natural Language Processing*, pages 2774–2779, 2017.

[31] Alon Talmor and Jonathan Berant. Multiqa: An empirical investigation of generalization and transfer in reading comprehension. *arXiv preprint arXiv:1905.13453*, 2019.

[32] Sebastian Zimmeck, Peter Story, Daniel Smullen, Abhilasha Ravichander, Ziqi Wang, Joel Reidenberg, N Cameron Russell, and Norman Sadeh. Maps: Scaling privacy compliance analysis to a million apps. *Proceedings on Privacy Enhancing Technologies*, 2019(3):66–86, 2019.

[33] Sebastian Zimmeck, Ziqi Wang, Lieyong Zou, Roger Iyengar, Bin Liu, Florian Schaub, Shomir Wilson, Norman Sadeh, Steven Bellovin, and Joel Reidenberg. Automated analysis of privacy requirements for mobile apps. In *2016 AAAI Fall Symposium Series*, 2016.

Differentially Private Language Models Benefit from Public Pre-training

Gavin Kerrigan*
University of California, Irvine
gavin.k@uci.edu

Dylan Slack*
University of California, Irvine
dslack@uci.edu

Jens Tuyls*
Princeton University
jtuyls@princeton.edu

Abstract

Language modeling is a keystone task in natural language processing. When training a language model on sensitive information, differential privacy (DP) allows us to quantify the degree to which our private data is protected. However, training algorithms which enforce differential privacy often lead to degradation in model quality. We study the feasibility of learning a language model which is simultaneously high-quality and privacy preserving by tuning a public base model on a private corpus. We find that DP fine-tuning boosts the performance of language models in the private domain, making the training of such models possible.[1]

1 Introduction

Language modeling, the task of assigning a probability to sequences of words, is a key problem in natural language processing. Modern language models are data-driven, relying on a large corpus of text. Many such models are trained on corpora from a specific domain, such as Wikipedia or news articles (Radford et al., 2019a). These models often suffer from generalization issues when used to model language from a different domain. This motivates the use of model fine-tuning, in which the weights of a pre-trained language model are tuned by gradient descent on a second dataset of interest (Radford et al., 2019a; Devlin et al., 2019; Liu et al., 2019).

In some cases, we would like to fine-tune our model with respect to a dataset containing private information. As such, there is an obligation to preserve the privacy of individuals who contribute text to the private training corpus. For example, training a medical chat-bot may require learning a language model from transcribed patient-doctor conversations; it would be critical that this model not expose sensitive information about the patients whose conversations are used as training data. In recent years, differential privacy (DP) has been a key quantitative measure of privacy which allows one to use aggregate statistical information about a dataset while preserving the privacy of its individual datapoints.

In the case of language modeling, we are interested in preserving the privacy of individuals who contribute text to a private corpus. As each individual who contributes to this dataset could potentially contribute several sentences, our notion of privacy is *group differential privacy* (Dwork and Roth, 2014), in which all sentences from a single individual are grouped. In practice, group DP is equivalent to DP with re-scaled parameters.A potential limitation of this approach is that the number of contributed sentences may not be uniform over users, leading to sub-optimal bounds on the privacy guarantee. There has been some success in directly training differentially private language models, but these often require access to large datasets in order to achieve a reasonable level of quality (McMahan et al., 2017). Other work has trained a differentially private base model which was then fine-tuned through active learning on a non-private dataset (Zhao et al., 2019).

We instead train a non-private base model on a large, public dataset, which we proceed to fine-tune on a private out-of-distribution dataset through differentially private stochastic gradient descent (DPSGD) (Abadi et al., 2016). By doing so, we successfully train a high-quality model which is differentially private with respect to our tuning dataset. Our experimental results show that DP fine-tuning not only boosts the performance of DP language modeling, but makes it possible.

*All authors contributed equally.

[1] https://github.com/dylan-slack/Finetuning-DP-Language-Models

Proceedings of the Second Workshop on Privacy in Natural Language Processing, pages 39–45
Online, Nov 20, 2020 ©2020 Association for Computational Linguistics
https://doi.org/10.18653/v1/P17

2 Related Work

Training a feedforward neural network with DP is achievable through the popular DP-SGD algorithm (Abadi et al., 2016). However, this method may lead to significant decreases in the accuracy (or other metrics) of the resulting model. Recent work considers the use of metric privacy for language modeling (Fernandes et al., 2019; Feyisetan et al., 2020), which is a relaxation of differential privacy where noise is instead added to the vector embedding of a word. We leave the exploration of metric privacy for the private fine-tuning task as a direction for future work.

Many high-quality language models rely on some form of recurrent neural architecture, such as RNNs or LSTMs (Sherstinsky, 2018; Hochreiter and Schmidhuber, 1997). In (McMahan et al., 2017), the authors develop a method for training such models while achieving differential privacy. However, this approach requires a large private dataset, and the mechanisms to achieve privacy lead to a significant decrease in model quality.

In (Zhao et al., 2019), the authors attempt to train a language model which is simultaneously differentially private and of high quality. The first solution proposed in (Zhao et al., 2019) is to fine-tune the language model with publicly available data, but as this public data is likely distributed differently than the private data, the resulting model is likely mistuned. The second proposed approach is to augment the training data by actively selecting non-private data instances. This effectively reduces the privacy cost incurred during each training step, but still requires training with potentially out-of-distribution data.

In contrast, our work begins with a pre-trained model which only has access to publicly available data. This base model is then fine-tuned through DPSGD on our private domain of interest, resulting in a model that is both differentially private and tuned with respect to our protected dataset. By tuning a pre-trained public model, we achieve higher quality models without incurring any additional costs to our privacy budget.

3 Approach

Let $\mathcal{D}$ be a publicly available corpus, and $\mathcal{P}$ be a protected corpus whose contents we would like to protect the privacy of. Denote by $\mathcal{X}$ the fixed, shared vocabulary of these corpora. At a high level, our approach is to first train a language model $M_{\mathcal{D}} : \mathcal{X}^n \to [0, 1]$. In practice, we choose a feedforward architecture for $M_{\mathcal{D}}$ due to limited computing resources. We fine-tune this model with respect to $\mathcal{P}$ by using the DPSGD algorithm (Abadi et al., 2016) on batches of sentences from $\mathcal{P}$.

3.1 (ϵ, δ) Differential Privacy

Intuitively, an algorithm is (ϵ, δ)-DP if the output of the algorithm cannot be used to probabilistically determine the presence of a single instance in the database by more than a factor of $\exp(\epsilon)$. We additionally allow this constraint to be violated with probability δ, with δ typically being small[2].

In the case of language modeling, an individual i may possibly contribute $s_i \geq 1$ sentences to the private training corpus. To maintain the privacy of said individual, we require that our algorithm satisfy *s_i-group differential privacy*, meaning our algorithm cannot be used to determine the presence or absence of s_i sentences in the dataset. However, (ϵ, δ) s_i-group DP is equivalent to $(\epsilon/s_i, \delta)$-DP (Dwork and Roth, 2014). Hence, it is sufficient to consider the somewhat unintuitive notion of preserving the privacy of individual sentences in the training set. Any mechanism satisfying (ϵ, δ)-DP on individual sentences will then satisfy $(\epsilon/\gamma, \delta)$-DP with respect to contributing individuals, where $\gamma = \max_i\{s_i\}$. Formally, an algorithm $\mathcal{A}$ satisfies (ϵ, δ)-DP if for all datasets $\mathcal{D}_1, \mathcal{D}_2$ differing by at most one instance, and for any set S, we have

$$\mathbb{P}\{\mathcal{A}(\mathcal{D}_1) \in S\} \leq \exp(\epsilon)\mathbb{P}\{\mathcal{A}(\mathcal{D}_2) \in S\} + \delta$$

Smaller ϵ values indicate a stronger privacy guarantee. We typically think of S being some query on the outcome of $\mathcal{A}$. A more complete treatment of differential privacy is available in (Dwork and Roth, 2014).

3.2 Differentially Private Fine-tuning

Differential privacy is achieved in SGD by adding appropriately scaled noise to the gradient of the loss function. In particular, we fix a noise scale $\sigma^2 \in \mathbb{R}$ and a gradient clipping level $C \in \mathbb{R}$. For a batch of size L, our loss function is given by $\mathcal{L}(\theta) = \frac{1}{L}\sum_i \mathcal{L}(x_i; \theta)$. For each x_i in our batch, we compute the clipped gradient $g(x_i)$ by scaling the gradient of the loss at x_i to have ℓ_2 norm at most C (Dwork and Roth, 2014).

[2]Some authors recommend a value of 10^{-5} (Abadi et al., 2016).

$$g(x_i) = \frac{1}{\max\{1, ||\nabla_\theta \mathcal{L}(x_i;\theta)||_2/C\}} \nabla_\theta \mathcal{L}(x_i;\theta)$$

We add appropriately scaled zero-mean Gaussian noise to our gradients:

$$\widetilde{g}(x_i) = g(x_i) + \mathcal{N}(0, \sigma^2 C^2 I)$$

Our gradient signal used in training is then the average of $\widetilde{g}(x_i)$ over a given mini-batch, which we use to determine a descent direction as in SGD. Note that our noisy gradient is equal to the true gradient in expectation, as we add mean-zero noise.

As our access to the private data is done entirely in the calculation of $g(x_i)$, with appropriately chosen parameters this method guarantees our algorithm respects our specified level of privacy.

For given noise σ, we can determine an acceptable privacy violation level $\delta \ll 1$ and compute the resulting privacy parameter ϵ through the composition theorem proved in (Abadi et al., 2016). In appendix B 2, we plot the (ϵ, δ)-privacy guarantees for various settings of σ. As expected, for a fixed δ, more noise (greater σ) results in a tighter privacy guarantee (smaller ϵ).

Throughout this section, we have assumed a maximum individual contribution size of $\gamma = 1$. When $\gamma > 1$, the only necessary change is a post-processing scaling of $\epsilon \mapsto \epsilon/\gamma$, as ϵ is computed based on parameters which are independent of γ.

4 Experimental Results

4.1 Datasets

For our public dataset, we choose the Brown corpus (Francis and Kucera, 1979), as it is a fairly large corpus designed to represent modern English. For our private dataset, we used the Reddit comments dataset (Reddit, 2019). While this corpus is not truly private, we felt it represented the type of language data one might be interested in protecting – written language generated by individual users which likely contains personal information. We randomly select a subset of 10k comments for private training data and 5k comments for development and testing. For more details, see Appendix C.

4.2 Models and Evaluation

For our language models, we consider two feed-forward architectures: a small network and a large network, each with three hidden layers, but with varying numbers of nodes (see appendix A for details). For both architectures, we train three baseline models:

- A non-private model trained only on the public corpus.
- A non-private model trained only on the private corpus.
- A non-private model pre-trained on the public corpus, and fine-tuned on the private corpus.

For each architecture, we compare these baseline models to a private model which is pre-trained on the public corpus and fine-tuned on the private corpus. For the private models, we hold $\delta = 1e{-}5$ and set gradient clipping to 1.0. We train each private model with $\sigma = 1.1$ and $\sigma = 0.1$. Also, we fine-tune OpenAI's pre-trained GPT-2 (Radford et al., 2019b) non-privately on both Brown and Reddit. For each model, we report the perplexity scores.

4.3 Results

GPT-2 Fine-tuning The GPT-2 model fine-tuned for three epochs on the Brown training data set scored 40.0 perplexity on the held out test set. The GPT-2 model fine-tuned for the same time on the Reddit training data set scored 45.14 on the held out test set.

Small Feedforward Neural Network Next, we trained and evaluated a smaller feedforward neural network on the evaluation schema from section 4.2. Figure 1(a) shows the test-set perplexity for each of our models as a function of training iterations. We observe that each of the base non-private models converges at roughly the same rate, but the models trained on the Brown corpus converge to a lower perplexity than those trained on the Reddit corpus. We also note that the fine-tuned models achieve a significantly lower perplexity in fewer iterations, even with the inclusion of differential privacy mechanisms. The increase in perplexity seen in the base Reddit model may be indicative of overfitting.

Large Feedforward Neural Network Next, we train and evaluate a large feedforward neural network model. The results can be found in figure 1(b). We found that the larger models performed mostly similar to the smaller ones. However, the larger model does significantly outperform its smaller counterpart when trained and evaluated on 10,000 comments sampled from the Reddit dataset. This can be seen when comparing figure 1(a) and 1(b). The "Reddit_10k / Reddit_10k" curve reaches a

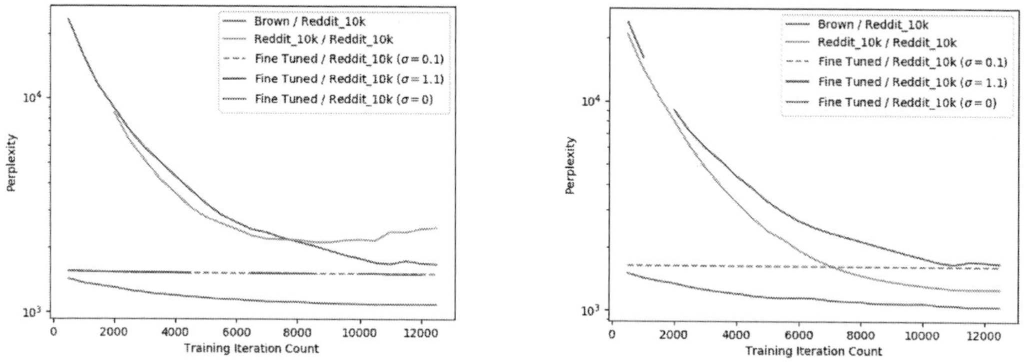

(a) Small Language Model

(b) Large Language Model

Figure 1: **Test-set perplexity as a function of training iterations for the small (a) and large (b) language models.** The legend indicates train-set / evaluation set, with σ being the noise scale used in differentially private training. The fine-tuned models are trained on the Brown corpus and tuned on the Reddit dataset. The graph for $\sigma = 1.1$ for the large language model is not visible since all perplexity values are infinity. Note: the graphs are truncated to the first epoch of training. Perplexities change marginally after this point.

much lower value much sooner for the larger model. Another difference is that the larger model was not able to get finite perplexity values when fine-tuned on Reddit_10k in a differentially private way with noise set to 1.1, while the smaller model was able to do this.

5 Analysis

Finetuning improves DP perplexity We summarize the perplexities of our final small and large models in table 1 in the appendix. A σ^2 of zero indicates non-private training while a $\sigma^2 > 0$ indicates private training where privacy increases with larger σ^2. We additionally provide the ϵ values for the private models in figure 4. The perplexity scores for both the small and large feedforward language models are orders of magnitude worse than the GPT-2 models indicating that they are not competitive with state of the art language models.

However, our results indicate that pre-training may significantly improve the perplexity of a differentially private language model. We were unsuccessful in training a differentially private model on the Reddit data alone, as all models tested gave unreasonably high perplexities (i.e. useless models). When DP fine-tuning was used to create a private language model for this domain, our small model outperformed the baseline models (except for its non-private equivalent). This indicates that pre-training may be highly valuable in facilitating the training of DP language models.

Qualitative Analysis We provide a sample of sentences generated from models fine-tuned on the Reddit $10k$ data set in table 2 in the appendix.

Aside from the state of the art GPT-2 model, both the small and large feedforward neural networks are not able to generate sentences that are coherent. Additionally, there is not a discernible difference between the various levels of private fine-tuning. This is likely because feedforward neural networks are not strong language models. We do see the pre-training benefits for privacy with such models.

6 Conclusions

Training neural models with differential privacy often significantly degrades model performance. However, differential privacy could prove crucial when doing language modeling on private datasets. Our work shows that DP fine-tuning not only boosts the performance of DP language modeling, but makes it possible. We also compared our experiments across two different model sizes and found that increasing the model size while decreasing the number of training epochs does not significantly impact the results in the differentially private transfer learning scenario. Future research could experiment with stronger model architectures (e.g., LSTM's, transformers) instead of regular feedforward neural networks, as well as train models longer in order to increase performance.

References

Martín Abadi, Andy Chu, Ian Goodfellow, H. Brendan McMahan, Ilya Mironov, Kunal Talwar, and Li Zhang. 2016. Deep Learning with Differential Privacy. *arXiv e-prints*, page arXiv:1607.00133.

J. Devlin, Ming-Wei Chang, Kenton Lee, and Kristina Toutanova. 2019. Bert: Pre-training of deep bidirectional transformers for language understanding. In *NAACL-HLT*.

Cynthia Dwork and Aaron Roth. 2014. The algorithmic foundations of differential privacy. *Found. Trends Theor. Comput. Sci.*, 9(3–4):211–407.

Natasha Fernandes, Mark Dras, and Annabelle McIver. 2019. Generalised differential privacy for text document processing. In *International Conference on Principles of Security and Trust*, pages 123–148. Springer, Cham.

Oluwaseyi Feyisetan, Borja Balle, Thomas Drake, and Tom Diethe. 2020. Privacy-and utility-preserving textual analysis via calibrated multivariate perturbations. In *Proceedings of the 13th International Conference on Web Search and Data Mining*, pages 178–186.

W. N. Francis and H. Kucera. 1979. Brown corpus manual. Technical report, Department of Linguistics, Brown University, Providence, Rhode Island, US.

Sepp Hochreiter and Jürgen Schmidhuber. 1997. Long short-term memory. *Neural Comput.*, 9(8):1735–1780.

Zhuohan Li, Eric Wallace, Sheng Shen, Kevin Lin, Kurt Keutzer, Dan Klein, and Joseph E. Gonzalez. 2020. Train large, then compress: Rethinking model size for efficient training and inference of transformers. *arXiv preprint arXiv:2002.11794*.

Y. Liu, Myle Ott, Naman Goyal, Jingfei Du, Mandar Joshi, Danqi Chen, Omer Levy, M. Lewis, L. Zettlemoyer, and V. Stoyanov. 2019. Roberta: A robustly optimized bert pretraining approach. *ArXiv*, abs/1907.11692.

H. Brendan McMahan, Daniel Ramage, Kunal Talwar, and Li Zhang. 2017. Learning differentially private language models without losing accuracy. *CoRR*, abs/1710.06963.

Alec Radford, Jeff Wu, Rewon Child, David Luan, Dario Amodei, and Ilya Sutskever. 2019a. Language models are unsupervised multitask learners.

Alec Radford, Jeffrey Wu, Rewon Child, David Luan, Dario Amodei, and Ilya Sutskever. 2019b. Language models are unsupervised multitask learners.

Reddit. 2019. May 2015 reddit comments.

Alex Sherstinsky. 2018. Fundamentals of recurrent neural network (RNN) and long short-term memory (LSTM) network. *CoRR*, abs/1808.03314.

Chris Waites. 2019. Pyvacy: Privacy algorithms for pytorch. `https://github.com/ChrisWaites/pyvacy`.

Zhengli Zhao, Nicolas Papernot, Sameer Singh, Neoklis Polyzotis, and Augustus Odena. 2019. Improving differentially private models with active learning.

A Architectures

We consider two language model architectures. We first use a feedforward neural network as our language model with three hidden layers consisting of 500, 250, and 50 nodes respectively ("small" language model). Recent work suggests large language models may produce better results more quickly than smaller models (Li et al., 2020). Though the mentioned work considers transformer models, we also investigate training a larger feedforward neural network with three hidden layers consisting of $10,000$, $5,000$, and $1,000$ nodes ("large" language model) in hopes to speed up differentially private training and gain better performance.

For both models, we consider 20 previous tokens. We trained the public models using the Adam optimizer with a learning rate of $1e-3$. To train the private models we used the DPSGD optimizer from (Waites, 2019). We used the ReLU activation function on all nodes and the softmax function on the output layer.

Lastly, we trained the small language model for 5 epochs during pre-training and 5 epochs during fine-tuning. We trained the large language model for 2 epochs during pre-training and 2 epochs during fine-tuning

B $(\epsilon-\delta)$-Privacy Guarantees

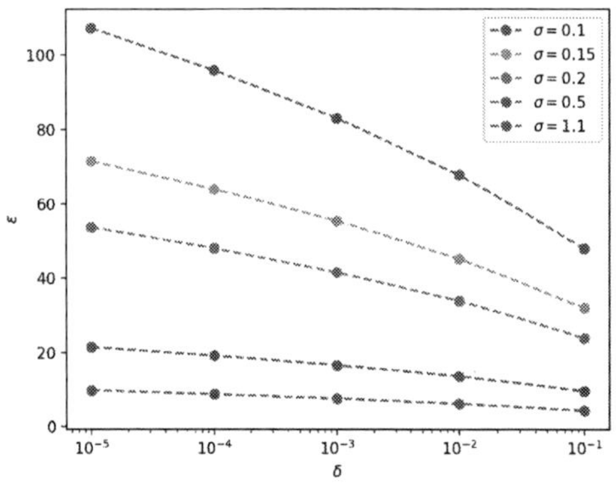

Figure 2: (ϵ, δ)-privacy guarantees for $q = 10^{-3}, T = 10^5$, computed using the moments accountant (Abadi et al., 2016). Here, σ is a noise-scale parameter specified by the user. This helps us to select a noise scale appropriate to a given application setting.

C Dataset Sizes

In figure 3, we provide the number of tokens used for training in each data set.

Dataset	Tokens (train)	Tokens (test)
Reddit_10k	689,763	344,120
Brown	693,683	-

Figure 3: The number of tokens in the training and test set of each dataset. Since we don't test on Brown, this entry is left empty.

D Additional Results

	Test Perplexity	
(σ^2, ϵ)	Small	Large
$(0.1, 107.30)$	1480.84	1627.56
$(1.1, 9.75)$	1473.49	NA

Figure 4: We provide the trade off between ϵ and test perplexity for the small and large models from figure 1. We hold δ to $1e-5$ and set the gradient clipping to 1.0. We include the lowest test perplexity for each model. Recall the large model with $\sigma = 1.1$ never converged to finite perplexity and is denoted NA.

Training / Testing Set	σ^2	PP (dev)	PP (test)	PP (dev, large)	PP (test, large)
Brown / Reddit_10k	0	1561.20	1584.54	1652.65	1677.42
Reddit_10k / Reddit_10k	0	3805.83	3787.68	1254.48	1259.23
fine-tuned / Reddit_10k	0.0	1035.45	1037.81	1016.65	1019.31
fine-tuned / Reddit_10k	0.1	1457.94	1480.84	1604.42	1627.56
fine-tuned / Reddit_10k	1.1	1450.01	1473.48	inf	inf

Table 1: Final test-set perplexities for each of our models. Fine-tuned refers to the model being trained on Brown, then fine-tuned on the Reddit 10K training set. PP marked as "large" are from the second, larger neural network we trained. Note that $\sigma^2 = 0.0$ refers to a non-DP model while $\sigma^2 > 0.0$ is a DP model, where the privacy guarantee increases with σ^2.

Model	Prompt	Sentence
Reddit_10k / Reddit_10k $\sigma^2 = 0.0$	"Bob lives close to the"	"know extent better though about really said breaking will"
fine-tuned / Reddit_10k $\sigma^2 = 0.0$	"Bob lives close to the"	"few alone saw good up done could branch clever been"
fine-tuned / Reddit_10k $\sigma^2 = 0.1$	"Bob lives close to the"	"city plans increase whose even reached years relieved construed what."
fine-tuned / Reddit_10k $\sigma^2 = 1.1$	"Bob lives close to the"	"along supply am certain like alone before decent exceeding other"
Large Reddit_10k / Reddit_10k $\sigma^2 = 0.0$	"Bob lives close to the"	"above twice wanted therefore while unless however defective."
Large fine-tuned / Reddit_10k $\sigma^2 = 0.0$	"Bob lives close to the"	"once obviously give found now re like exact dislike out."
Large fine-tuned / Reddit_10k $\sigma^2 = 0.1$	"Bob lives close to the"	"leaders kid forward governor thought neck let rides orchestral should"
fine-tuned GPT-2 / Reddit_10k	"Bob lives close to the"	"station and we only have two miles of travel left to go"

Table 2: A selection of sentences generated from the prompt "Bob lives close" using models finetuned on the Reddit $10k$ data set. Except for the GPT-2 model, there's not a strong difference between the coherency of sentences generated.

Association for Computational Linguistics
209 N. Eighth Street
Stroudsburg, Pennsylvania 18360

ISBN 978-1-7138-2001-7

9 781713 820017

CURRAN ASSOCIATES INC.
proceedings.com